D1010808

THE WORLD'S GREATEST BOOK

THE STORY *of* HOW THE BIBLE CAME TO BE

LAWRENCE H. SCHIFFMAN, PH.D.
& JERRY PATTENGALE, PH.D.
GENERAL EDITORS
with LEN WOODS

WORLD'S GREATEST BOOK: The Story of How the Bible Came to Be

Published by Worthy Books, an imprint of Worthy Publishing Group, a division of Worthy Media, Inc., One Franklin Park, 6100 Tower Circle, Suite 210, Franklin, TN 37067, in association with Museum of the Bible.

WORTHY is a registered trademark of Worthy Media, Inc.

HELPING PEOPLE EXPERIENCE THE HEART OF GOD

eBook available wherever digital books are sold.

Library of Congress Control Number: 2017947428

Image credits for the color pages. *First set:* Alamy (pages 2, 4, 5); Commons.Wikimedia.org (pages 6, 7); Everett Collection (page 8); Shutterstock (pages 1, 3, 5). *Second set:* Alamy (pages 1, 3, 4, 5, 7); Commons.Wikimedia.org (pages 2, 7); Everett Collection (page 6); Museum of the Bible Collection (page 8); Westminster College, Cambridge (page 7).

Front cover image credits: Top image: iStock, 139738413 Bottom images, left to right: "William Tyndale" - Classic Image / Alamy Stock Photo; "Torah Scroll" – Green Collection private collection; "Saint Jerome in His Study" - ART Collection / Alamy Stock Photo

Cover Design: David Carlson, Gilbert & Carlson Design

Produced with the assistance of Hudson Bible (www.HudsonBible.com)

ISBN: 978-1945470011

Printed in the USA

1 2 3 4 5 6 7 8 9 SB 22 21 20 19 18 17

To Michael Cromartie, whose Faith Angle Forum for decades has gathered key journalists and thought leaders from various backgrounds. And all of this in the hope of understanding better the Bible's message and its various faith traditions. His magnetic joy and journey evoke hope, and he helps us to realize that a rigorous thought life can lead to good things.

To the International Jewish Committee for Interreligious Consultations (IJCIC) for its leadership in fostering interfaith harmony between international bodies of faith communities, and for the opportunity to work together with Jewish and Christian colleagues who are devoted to spreading the message of mutual respect and cooperation that is the goal of our respective communities.

And to the Green family (founders of Hobby Lobby stores) for their strategic role in establishing the Museum of the Bible. Also, to the many thousands of others who have already joined them in this journey.

CONTENTS

PREFACE

The story you are about to read has many twists and turns, heroes and heroines, and exciting episodes of confrontation and intrigue. Throughout, our story is propelled by generations of devoted scholars who have worked to transmit the "world's greatest book" throughout the generations from antiquity to modern times.

What makes this story more engaging is that it is based on historical sources—all true to the best of our knowledge. We would neither have dedicated our time and effort to this project, nor agreed to the book's title, if we did not agree that the story told here is of enormous importance to our culture and civilization.

We hope you enjoy reading this book as much as we enjoyed working on it. It is the second book we have produced together—the coming together of a Jewish scholar who practices his faith, and a Christian scholar who does the same, both of whom are dedicated to the highest standards of academic scholarship. We both have worked for religious and nonreligious organizations, both internationally and locally, and have spent considerable time in Israel as well. While we recognize that we have differences regarding some key matters, we also appreciate our important commonalities and our agreement regarding the role that the Bible (whether the Hebrew Bible or the Christian Bible) has played in the past and that it can continue to play in the future.

We also thank our colleague, Len Woods, who helped merge our thoughts and words. We began planning this book in the Skirball Department of Hebrew and Judaic Studies at New York University, after which Len drafted a manuscript. Through the following months of exchanges, we revised and discussed hundreds of topics and historical pivots until we arrived at this text. We were informed recently that the number of preordered copies is higher than many books' final sales—a tribute to the subject matter and to the continued work of Len, various experts weighing in, and our partners at Worthy Publishing.

—Lawrence H. Schiffman and Jerry A. Pattengale

WHAT'S SO GREAT ABOUT THE BIBLE?

The book to read is not the
one which thinks for you,
but the one which makes you think.
No book in the world equals the Bible for that.

—Harper Lee, author, *To Kill a Mockingbird*

With a light rain falling on Manhattan's Upper East Side and a windchill near freezing, it was hardly an ideal night for an auction.

Yet none of that mattered to the eager buyers who crowded into Sotheby's, New York, on November 26, 2013. The sought-after prize? One of two copies of *The Bay Psalm Book* owned by the Old South Church in Boston. In 1640, this collection of biblical psalms had been translated from Hebrew and then typeset and printed by Puritan settlers. It was the first book published in British North America, just twenty years after the landing of the *Mayflower*.

Of the 1,700 copies originally printed, only eleven are known to survive.

Just two and a half minutes after an opening bid of $6 million, frenzied buyers were offering more than $12 million for this rare piece of religious history! The final purchase price was $14.165 million, earning *The Bay Psalm Book* the new world record for the most expensive printed book ever sold at auction.

Mind-boggling, isn't it? And yet—antiquities experts are quick to point out—if you think *that's* pricey, consider the Gutenberg Bible. One leaf (a single sheet, made up of two pages) from a Gutenberg Bible can sell for as much as $100,000. This is because the Gutenberg Bible is the first major book ever printed using movable type. What's more, it predates *The Bay Psalm Book* by more than 180 years! Of the forty-eight copies of the Gutenberg Bible that remain, only thirty-one are said to be in excellent condition. In the summer of 2015, eight leaves (including the Old Testament book of Esther) were auctioned at Sotheby's for just under $1 million. Experts estimate that if an entire Gutenberg Bible ever came up for auction, it would likely fetch upward of $50 million!

These are not isolated instances. In May 2014, at Christie's in Paris, an Italian Torah scroll (the first five books of the Hebrew and Christian Bibles) sold for a record $3.87 million.

In early December 2016, the extensive private Bible collection of the late Dr. Charles Ryrie, a biblical scholar and longtime professor at Dallas Theological Seminary, sold at Sotheby's for $7.34 million. His Wycliffe Bible alone brought in $1.4 million.

Why do people attach such immense value to a bunch of old religious writings?

To be fair, not everyone does.

If you could time-travel back to Berlin, Germany, on the afternoon of November 9, 1938, you would arrive just in time for *Kristallnacht*, the infamous "Night of Broken Glass."

This is the night the violence of the Holocaust was unleashed. A firestorm of racist rage—encouraged by Nazi government officials—broke out against Jews living throughout the German Reich. When the smoke cleared, ninety-one Jews were dead, hundreds more were injured, thousands of Jewish businesses and homes had been vandalized, and some 250 synagogues lay in smoldering ruins. In the days to come, Jewish men would be rounded up by the tens of thousands, put on trains, and shipped off to concentration camps.

Unreported in most history books is how much anger on *Kristallnacht* was also directed against the Hebrew Bible. In many cases, before setting a synagogue ablaze, mobs first removed its Torah scrolls. They piled these scrolls in nearby streets or parks and ceremoniously burned them while onlookers cackled, clapped, and danced around the flames. In some places, Nazi officials made rabbis incinerate their Torah scrolls before forcing them to read aloud from Hitler's *Mein Kampf.*

In other cities, the revered Hebrew writings weren't burned; they were ripped apart. In Vienna, Austria, Torah scraps were tied to the backs of terrified Jews, who were then chased down city streets. One witness reported seeing German children marching gleefully atop a pile of shredded Torahs.

The carnage on this night was creative in its cruelty. In Fritzlar, Germany, the synagogue's sacred scrolls were taken to Nikolaus Street and unrolled so that a group of Hitler Youth could ride their bicycles over them. In Bavarian Lichtenfeld, when a Jewish woman tried to halt the desecration of sacred writings, she was accosted by several children. Following a brief struggle, the woman was dead. Children took the synagogue's prayer books and used them to play an impromptu game of football.[1]

Throughout much of recorded history, one can find fierce antagonism toward the Bible. Around 600 BCE, the irate King Jehoiakim of Judah cut and burned a sacred scroll from the Jewish prophet Jeremiah (Jeremiah 36). In 303 BCE, the Roman emperor Diocletian issued an edict calling for the eradication of all Christian writings throughout the Roman Empire. More recently, ISIS extremists in Mosul, Iraq, have been videotaped burning piles of Bibles.

It seems the adage is true: one man's trash is another man's treasure.

And vice versa.

When it comes to the Bible, everyone has an opinion. America's sixteenth president, Abraham Lincoln, gushed that the Bible was "the best gift God has given to man" and that "all the good the Savior gave to the world was communicated through this Book."[2]

Compare Lincoln's warm sentiments to the decidedly colder view of Celsus, a philosopher of Platonism in the second century. He called the Jewish and Christian Bibles "altogether absurd."[3] Seventeen centuries later, American novelist Mark Twain wrote that the Bible contains "some good morals; and a wealth of obscenity; and upwards of a thousand lies."[4] More recently, British actor Ian McKellen said on the *Today* show, "I've often thought the Bible should have a disclaimer in the front saying, 'This is fiction.'"[5]

Surely a book this discussed and disputed, this revered and reviled is worth a closer look.

This is a book about one of the world's most loved and loathed books. Given that, we should probably begin with some definitions and distinctions—and at least a few disclaimers.

What do we mean when we speak of the *Bible*? Our English word comes from the ancient Greek word *biblion* (plural, *biblia*), which means "scroll" or "book." It is related to the Greek word *biblos*, the name given to Egyptian papyrus shipped from the Phoenician port city of Byblos to Greece.

Over time, ancient Jews and early Christians began to use the word *biblia*, or Bible, to refer to a specific collection of writings that they deemed sacred. Common synonyms for the Bible include Scripture, Holy Writ, the Word of God, and the Good Book.

The Bible is one book made up of many smaller books. Jerome, a fourth-century scholar best known for translating the Bible into Latin, called the Bible "the Divine Library."[6] What are the books that make up this "Divine Library"? The answer to that question depends on whom you ask.

The *Hebrew Bible* contains twenty-four books, divided into three categories: the five books of Moses, known also by the Hebrew term *Torah*; the eight books of the Prophets, also known as the *Nevi'im*; and the eleven books of the Writings, also known as the *Ketuvim*. All together, these books are referred to as the *Tanakh* (an acronym formed from the first letters—T, N, K—of those section titles).

The three divisions of the Hebrew Bible are arranged roughly chronologically. The Torah was canonized first, and it appears as a unified corpus in the Hebrew Bible. The Prophets were collected next, brought to a close after the last of the prophets: Haggai, Zechariah, and Malachi. Earlier nonprophetic works, such as Psalms, Proverbs, and Job, as well as works completed after the prophets, were collected in the Writings.

The *Protestant Bible* contains all twenty-four books of the Hebrew Bible. However, it counts some of the longer books that both Jews and Christians divide into two parts as separate books, for a total of thirty-nine books, and arranges them in a different order. Instead of referring to these books as the Tanakh, Christians call them the *Old Testament.*

The word *testament* means "covenant" or "agreement." A last will and testament, for example, is a legally binding agreement specifying the distribution of one's property and possessions. Like Jews, Christians see the books of the Hebrew Bible as the story of how the agreement God made with the Jewish patriarch Abraham unfolded through the time of Moses, the kings, and the prophets.

To this collection of books, all written before the Common Era, Christians add twenty-seven more books, written during the mid-to-late first century CE. Christians call these books the *New Testament,* believing that they signal a new era in how God relates to Jews and non-Jews.

Christians see the Gospels (the first four books of the New Testament) as reliable accounts of the life and ministry of Jesus of Nazareth. Because of his recorded words and works, Christians believe Jesus to be the *Messiah* (the mighty deliverer/king) promised by the Old Testament prophets. They see the book of Acts as the story of the birth and growth of the church, the Epistles (letters) as instructions for the people of God, and the book of Revelation as a prophecy about the end of this present age. Thus, the Hebrew Bible has only twenty-four books, while the Protestant Bible contains sixty-six.

What about the *Catholic Bible* and the *Eastern Orthodox Bible*? Here, things get a bit trickier. These groups recognize the sixty-six books of the Protestant Bible, but they also include several additional books and extra passages that emerged from Jewish authors during the Second Temple period, often termed the "intertestamental era" by Christians (roughly 400 BCE to 1 CE).

While some Christians regard these extra writings (also called *deuterocanonical* or *apocryphal* writings) as sacred and inspired, others see them as merely useful or worth reading. Traditional Judaism forbade the reading of apocryphal texts, although occasional quotations of such texts appeared in rabbinic literature. However, modern times have seen an awakening of scholarly and popular interest in these works. In a later chapter, we will examine the criteria used by various religious bodies to determine whether a writing deserved to be called Scripture.

When all the book counting is complete, we are left with this: the Hebrew Bible recognizes twenty-four biblical books, the Protestant Bible sixty-six, the Catholic Bible seventy-three, and the Eastern Orthodox Bible eighty.

Many people are surprised to discover that reading the Bible is not at all like reading a self-help book or novel. From book to book (and sometimes even within a single book), the Bible shifts gears and switches genres. Its writings are, frankly, a mash-up of material. Stories are interspersed with teachings. In one place, you encounter detailed instructions about religious rituals. In another place, you find heart-stopping action. The Bible—with its quirky amalgamation of poetry, proverbs, parables, and prophetic literature, its public sermons and private correspondence, its genealogies and census records—is less like a modern book and more like an ancient scrapbook of Jewish and Christian history and beliefs.

So why would we call the Bible "the world's greatest book"? The Bible is controversial. Many passages are not easy to read or understand. And then there is the awful truth that terrible things—slavery and the subjugation of women, for example—have been justified throughout history by people citing the Bible!

It's a fair question. And there's no getting around it: horrible abuses have been perpetrated through the centuries by people claiming biblical support. But consider some other realities.

The Bible Has Been a Catalyst for Positive Social Change.

Throughout recorded history, the teaching of Scripture has inspired humanitarian efforts. There's no way to know how many hospitals and schools have been built or how many charitable nonprofits and food banks have been established because of the Bible's injunctions to care for strangers, orphans, and widows (Deuteronomy 24:17, 19) and to "love your neighbor" (Leviticus 19:18, echoed in Mark 12:31).

The same Bible that was used by some to justify slavery also prompted many in the abolitionist movement of the mid-1800s to denounce the practice and call for its end. Its teachings undergirded the powerful work of Dr. Martin Luther King Jr.—by profession a preacher of the Bible's message. Biblical references are woven throughout King's "I Have a Dream" speech, one of the most famous and influential in American history.

The Bible Has a One-Of-a-Kind History.
The Bible was penned by dozens of writers in three continents over a span of ten to fifteen centuries. That's admittedly unique. What other book has such a diverse background?

The Bible Possesses an Enduring Nature.
Throughout history there have been repeated attempts to discredit or destroy these writings considered to be sacred, but the Bible has survived each one. Countless people have perished in their efforts to defend and distribute the Bible.

The Bible Has Shaped Three World Religions.
Jews traditionally have accepted the books that comprise the Hebrew Bible. Christians have embraced both the Old Testament (Hebrew Bible) and New Testament. Muslims have adapted many of the stories and people from the Bible and included them in the Qur'an, though with changes from the earlier texts and with claims that Jews and Christians falsified aspects of the Bible. (It should be noted that centuries of careful textual study by thousands of scholars, comparing the earliest biblical texts with those of the seventh- and eighth-century Muslim assertions, do not support such claims.) All said, the Hebrew Bible became the important

foundational document for the Jews and, together with the New Testament, for the Christians. Several centuries later, both volumes became influential for the Muslims, though second to the Qur'an and through a distinctly Muslim lens.

The Bible Has Had a Monumental Influence on Western Culture. Consider some of the many ways that the Bible has influenced our culture and, indeed, all of Western civilization.

The Bible has been foundational in education.
Many of the world's oldest and most prestigious colleges and universities—such as Oxford, Cambridge, Harvard, and Yale—began as schools for training students in how to teach and preach the Bible. (Harvard and Yale were founded by the Puritans, the same group that published *The Bay Psalm Book*.)

The Bible permeates the halls of American government.
Bible verses are engraved or referenced on many public buildings—including the Jefferson and Lincoln Memorials—across Washington, DC. The cornerstone of the Washington Monument has a Bible deposited in it. A marble relief portrait of Moses, the great lawgiver of Israel, looks down on the House chamber in the US Capitol. The Library of Congress showcases a Gutenberg Bible in a prominent and permanent display, and several Bible verses (Psalm 19:1; Proverbs 4:7; Micah 6:8; John 1:5) are etched into its walls. Historians tell us that Psalm 35 was read at the first Continental Congress in 1774. And guess what? All these years later,

the Bible is *still* prominent in the American political process. The morning after the 2016 US presidential election, Democratic candidate Hillary Clinton quoted Galatians 6:9 in her concession speech. When Clinton's running mate, Tim Kaine, added a few words of appreciation, he alluded to a parable told by Jesus in Matthew 20:1–6 about workers laboring in a vineyard. A few weeks later, in his inauguration speech, America's forty-fifth president, Donald Trump, paraphrased Psalm 133:1.

The Bible has influenced the arts and entertainment.
Many of the world's most famous and exquisite works of art—such as Da Vinci's *The Last Supper* and Michelangelo's "The Creation of Adam" fresco and *David* sculpture—feature scriptural themes. Some of Hollywood's biggest blockbusters—*The Ten Commandments, Ben-Hur, The Passion of the Christ*—have strong biblical storylines.

The Bible has altered our language.
Many biblical phrases have become part of our everyday vernacular, such as *an eye for an eye, a thorn in the flesh, there's nothing new under the sun*, and *go the extra mile*. Thanks to the wildly popular King James Bible, we use hundreds of such phrases almost every day. Most people have no clue when they use these common idioms that they are quoting Scripture! Though our culture may not be Bible-centered, it is most certainly Bible-saturated. Even the avowed skeptic H. L. Mencken admitted about the King James Bible, "It is probably the most beautiful piece of writing in all the literature of the world."[7]

The Bible is history's best-selling book.

More than six billion copies of the Bible have been printed. Every year, an estimated 100 million copies of Scripture are sold—with no telling how many more copies are given away. One could counter that numbers alone aren't a reliable measure of greatness. After all, certain fast-food chains have sold billions of burgers, pizzas, and tacos . . . and no one is arguing that the lofty sales figures suggest these establishments are serving up gourmet fare. But though it's true that *quantity* by itself doesn't prove anything, clearly some *quality* of the Bible has motivated the making and acquiring of an incredible number of copies of it.

Before we get into our discussion of the Bible in the following chapters, a few disclaimers are in order.

The Bible was originally written in Hebrew, Aramaic, and Greek, so each time we cite a biblical statement in English, we are quoting a *translation* of the Bible. There are many good translations, each one attempting to render the original words of Scripture in an accurate, clear manner. In this book, we have decided to quote primarily from the New Revised Standard Version (NRSV).

However, on occasion you will come across references like this: (Exodus 25:3, NJPS). That's a reference to a translation other than the NRSV—in this case, the new (1985) translation of the Hebrew Bible from the Jewish Publication Society. The numbers in each reference function as an address. In this case, they are telling you to look at chapter 25 of the book of Exodus, specifically the third verse. The Bible's chapter divisions were added in the thirteenth century. Verse numbers were added later—to the Hebrew Bible around 1448 and the New Testament around 1551—to help readers navigate the text.

Since the Bible is a book about God, we will be mentioning God in this book. In doing so, we will follow the traditional custom of using masculine pronouns—he, his, him—to refer to deity. We do this not because we think God is male (several biblical passages ascribe feminine qualities to God, such as Isaiah 49:15, 66:13, and Hosea 13:8). We do this because the ancient biblical texts do this.

Let's be clear at the outset: this is not a book about the *content* or *message* of the Bible. Our goal is not to discuss or dismiss theological beliefs. Rather, this is a peek into the fascinating history of the Bible. This is the story behind what some refer to as "the greatest story ever told." How in the world did we get this book that some people swear by—and other people swear at?

The World's Greatest Book is meant to be a book for everyone. It is for the faithless and the faithful. You don't have to be a believer to admit that the Bible has played a significant role in human civilization. You also don't have to be a skeptic to have a grocery list of questions about the formation of the Bible, such as:

- Who wrote these documents and when?
- How were these ancient writings transmitted through the ages?

- As scribes made copies of copies, didn't they make mistakes that caused the ancient writings to be changed and corrupted?
- How was it decided which writings would be included in the Bible?
- What are the Dead Sea Scrolls, and why are archaeological finds like these such a big deal?

In this book, we hope to provide satisfying answers to those questions. Mostly, however, our goal—whether you are an agnostic from Amsterdam, a Jew living in Jerusalem, or a Christian from Canada—is for you to know the long and winding background of how the Bible came to be. It is a fascinating story that includes a little bit of everything: adventure and violence, mystery and bravery, and dumb luck or divine intervention, depending on your point of view.

We think everyone should know the remarkable story of the Bible—that the Torah you read on your smartphone using a Bible app required the efforts of kings and scholars, committees and councils, and a host of hardworking scribes . . . and that the reason there is a Gideon Bible in the drawer next to your hotel bed is that countless people over thousands of years wrote, copied, hid, copied, protected, copied, collated, compared, corrected, and copied some more . . . then searched, researched, studied, translated, smuggled, printed, shipped, and—in many cases—suffered or even died for it.

We want you to know that the production team of the Bible included not only prominent religious leaders but also an unlikely cast of offbeat characters. In these pages you will encounter, among others, an unsuspecting bedouin hunter, a couple of Scottish widows riding camels across North Africa, an astronaut, and a cheese merchant. Throw in a washing machine and a hunt for nutrient-rich soil, and we're pretty sure the story of how we got the Bible is a story you won't soon forget.

Issues of faith aside, veteran religion reporter Kenneth Briggs, formerly of the *New York Times*, was spot-on when he said, "The Bible is the springboard to opening all kinds of ideas, thoughts, beliefs about what our life is about."[8]

Welcome to the fascinating story of how we got the world's greatest book.

CHAPTER ONE

IN THE BEGINNING

Encounter at Sinai

The Lord came down on Mount Sinai,
to the top of the mountain;
and the Lord called Moses to the top of
the mountain, and Moses went up.
Then the Lord spoke to Moses.

—Exodus 19:20–21 NASB

In 1843 Dr. Constantin von Tischendorf, an instructor on leave from the University of Leipzig, grew weary of studying old texts in the musty libraries of Europe. So, he packed his bags and took off. This young German scholar with piercing eyes and a shock of dark, wavy hair had one goal: to discover and decipher the oldest surviving copies of Scripture. Tischendorf was obsessed, and he was relentless. He spent thirteen months in Italy before making his way to Egypt. He was Indiana Jones minus the bullwhip (and plus a serious set of pork-chop sideburns).

In 1844, Tischendorf arrived at Saint Catherine's (or, as it is officially known, the Holy Monastery of the God-Trodden Mount Sinai), an ancient Eastern Orthodox monastery built at the base of the mountain traditionally claimed to be Sinai, in modern-day Egypt. Perhaps while in Italy he had read of the experience of Vitaliano Donati, professor of botany and natural history at the University of Turin. Donati had himself visited Saint Catherine's in 1791.

As far as we know, Donati didn't make any significant botanical discoveries in the sands around Sinai. He did, however, spy a book that captured his attention. He wrote in his journal of having seen an old Bible at Saint Catherine's "comprising leaves of handsome, large, delicate, and square-shaped parchment, written in a round and handsome script."[1]

It may have been this reference that prompted the not-yet-thirty-year-old Tischendorf to cross the Mediterranean, trek hundreds of miles across the North African wilderness, and knock on the door of Saint Catherine's. At any rate, by coming to Sinai, he had come to the right place.

In a sense, the story of how the Bible came to be begins at Sinai. While the biblical stories start with creation, Adam and Eve, the

Flood, and the patriarchs (early Hebrew leaders who followed God), the same text says it was Moses who recorded this narrative.

Many within the Judeo-Christian tradition have suspected that it may have been in this place, where Saint Catherine's Monastery now sits, that God first called to Moses from the midst of a burning bush (Exodus 3:1–6). As a matter of fact, if you ever have the privilege of visiting, the monks of Saint Catherine's will gladly show you a bush growing—but not burning—in their courtyard. They believe this is the actual bush referred to in Scripture!

Tradition says that Moses followed this divine call and made a beeline to Pharaoh's palace. There, equipped with a miracle-working staff, assisted by his brother Aaron, and enabled by the power of God, Moses liberated the people of Israel from many generations of slavery. Then he led them on a two-month journey back to Mount Sinai (which some traditionalists think was also called Mount Horeb). As the people camped at the base, Moses met with God on the summit (Exodus 19:1–2). According to the Hebrew Bible (what Christians call the Old Testament), after receiving God's law, Moses descended the mountain. There, the Bible teaches, in the rocky valley beneath Sinai, Moses read these divine decrees to the Jewish people. This is the place where the people of Israel entered into a covenant relationship with God.

We can't afford to miss this fact: it is while the Jewish people were at Sinai that we find the first biblical references to "the book of the covenant" (Exodus 24:7). In other words, it is in this remote desert place that, according to Judeo-Christian tradition, the laws, words, and what the Israelites believed to be the pronouncements of God first began to be written down. Consider these verses from the book of Exodus—a passage that describes events that reportedly took place at Sinai:

- "Moses wrote down all the words of the Lord" (Exodus 24:4).
- "[Moses] took the book of the covenant, and read it in the hearing of the people; and they said, 'All that the Lord has spoken we will do, and we will be obedient'" (Exodus 24:7).
- "The Lord said to Moses, 'Come up to me on the mountain, and wait there; and I will give you the tablets of stone, with the law and the commandment, which I have written for their instruction'" (Exodus 24:12).
- "When God finished speaking with Moses on Mount Sinai, he gave him the two tablets of the covenant, tablets of stone, written with the finger of God" (Exodus 31:18).

The belief of Judeo-Christian tradition is that the Bible, as we know it, began at Sinai. God spoke (and even wrote on stone tablets) certain words, and it is believed that Moses did a good bit of writing too (Exodus 24:4; 34:28–29). This revelation has been understood by both Judaism and Christianity to be the beginning of the composition of the five books of Moses (Torah). The exact nature of that process, however, has long been debated by religious thinkers and scholars.

If old biblical writings were what Dr. Tischendorf hoped to find, then stopping at Saint Catherine's was the best decision he ever made. The monastery was renowned even in the 1840s for its vast, valuable library. (Today it is regarded as the oldest continually functioning library in the world!)

We should note that Tischendorf did *not* unearth any broken stone tablets (as described in Exodus 32:19) at Saint Catherine's. However, the professor *did* make a startling and important discovery. According to his version of events (which monastery officials vigorously dispute), Tischendorf noticed some parchments in a waste bin near the monastery's furnace.

The scholar retrieved them and examined them closely. They were large, measuring about 15 x 13.5 inches. They had four columns of text on each side. They were handwritten in beautiful uncial (all capital letters) script.

Even in the dim light, Tischendorf could see that the parchments were part of a codex, an ancient manuscript formatted like a modern book. He realized they were from a very old Septuagint (a Greek translation of the Old Testament). In all, Tischendorf counted 129 leaves (pages) that seemed destined to serve as kindling!

According to Dr. Bruce Metzger, a noted Greek and New Testament scholar, one of the monks informed the horrified Tischendorf that two such baskets of "rubbish" had already been burned. Unable to conceal his concern, the visitor asked if he might have the stash of discarded parchments.

Perhaps only then perceiving their value, the monks' mood changed. They eventually agreed to let Tischendorf take one-third (or forty-three) of the leaves.

To his lifelong delight, Tischendorf had acquired a portion of a 1,500-year-old Greek version of the Bible! Now known as Codex Sinaiticus ("the Sinai book," because of where it was discovered), this fourth-century manuscript is especially prized because it helps modern scholars see how their ancient colleagues labored to preserve the correct wording of the biblical text down through the centuries.

Back in Europe, Tischendorf donated these forty-three leaves to the Leipzig University Library, refusing to divulge where he had found them. In 1846, he published their contents—the Old Testament books 1 Chronicles, Jeremiah, Nehemiah, and Esther. Then he began to dream (and perhaps scheme) of returning to Saint Catherine's to acquire the rest.

Dr. Dirk Jongkind, former curator of the codex at the British Library, says it is easy to imagine Tischendorf's excitement, as these leaves are not only old but majestic. Jongkind recently finished an exhaustive project that utilized this ancient codex, among others, to produce a rich, interactive biblical text project, *The Greek New Testament, Produced at Tyndale House, Cambridge*. He describes an encounter with the great codex:

> Every time I see [it], the sheer size of the manuscript strikes me. Many Greek manuscripts are just fragments or have just one or perhaps even two columns; yet here we have four columns in the prose sections with generous margins all around. And then it quickly becomes clear how much this manuscript is an accumulation of many centuries of transmission history. The production phase with a team of different scribes is the oldest layer. Then you get a group of corrections that are made a few centuries later. You get medieval Arabic notes and some late Greek annotations all the way up to modern times with library stamps and folio numbers in pencil. The parchment is as thin as possible, the surface smooth, and, though some sections have suffered through the ages, the characteristics of good parchment have preserved most of the text in exquisite detail.[2]

How did we get from Moses receiving stone tablets at the top of Mount Sinai to Constantin von Tischendorf drooling over old parchments at the base of Sinai some three millennia later?

How did this book we call the Bible come to be?

Ask random people on the street that question, and in most cases, you will get blank stares and shoulder shrugs. Or you may hear such wildly imaginative answers as:

- "The Bible is a bunch of made-up stories that religious people claim to be revelations from God."
- "I'm not exactly sure, but I'm guessing angels were involved?"
- "At various times and places, God would start speaking out loud, and people like Moses and Paul would grab their writing utensils. They were like ancient secretaries. The process was like divine dictation."
- "The Spirit of God would come over people and put them into a spiritual trance. When this happened, they scribbled furiously the inspired thoughts they were having, as if they were channeling God."

People have all sorts of theories and ideas about *how* the Bible was written. The truth is, we are not sure exactly *how* this mysterious process worked. All we know is that the Bible purports to describe remarkable, divine encounters. And it claims to convey the very utterances of God. This is why, some 400 times in the Hebrew Bible, we find the phrase, "Thus says the LORD."

Another thing we don't know is how soon after the fact biblical events were recorded. Traditionalists believe that Moses was the human writer chiefly responsible for the first five books of the Hebrew Bible or Old Testament (known collectively as the Torah, Law, or Pentateuch). For them, this means that the process of Moses receiving and recording holy revelations began at Mount Sinai and continued for his remaining forty years of life. Between the events at Sinai and his final addresses to the Israelite people, Moses is said to have penned Genesis, Exodus, Leviticus, Numbers, and Deuteronomy.

Others, influenced by the nineteenth-century German scholar Julius Wellhausen, cite different writing styles and vocabularies throughout the Pentateuch. The idea behind what has been termed the *documentary hypothesis* is that these five biblical books were not penned by Moses between 1300 and 1200 BCE but were instead compiled by scribes between about 950 and 500 BCE. According to this theory, these writers relied on the nation's rich oral traditions and on written records that had been passed down by prior generations. (Considerable challenges have led to modification of specific details of the documentary hypothesis.)

Whichever view one takes about the authorship of the Pentateuch, two things are clear: Ancient Jewish culture, like other primitive and modern cultures, *did* tell, retell, and even memorize stories. And the ancient Hebrews could read, write, and keep records (Exodus 17:14; Deuteronomy 10:1–4; 27:2–3, 8; 31:19, 24–26). They recorded information—both important and trivial—for posterity. Archaeologists have found ancient Hebrew inscriptions on everything from walls to pottery.

To a degree, these realities make moot the question of when the original documents of Scripture came into existence. Before literacy was widespread, and even after it became common, history was preserved orally, via stories. This is how values were transmitted, how cultures bonded, and how people were entertained.

Can you picture a group of nomadic people clustered around a desert campfire at night as they sing a song about a great victory over an enemy tribe? Can you imagine them as they listen to a sage tell tales of ancient heroes? If so, then you have a good sense of how parts of the Hebrew Bible may have been passed down before they were put into written form. The book of Exodus describes Moses and the people preserving their history in this way: "Then Moses and the Israelites sang this song to the LORD" (Exodus 15:1).

The Bible records another example of this kind of ancient recordkeeping (or remembering) in Jeremiah 36. God tells the prophet Jeremiah, "Take a scroll and write on it all the words that I have spoken to you against Israel and Judah and all the nations, from the day I spoke to you, from the days of Josiah until today" (Jeremiah 36:2).

This command implies that the prophet had either a remarkable memory or some kind of careful, written record of prior revelations. Perhaps it was a bit of both. Jeremiah summoned his secretary: "Jeremiah called Baruch son of Neriah, and Baruch wrote on a scroll at Jeremiah's dictation all the words of the LORD that he had spoken to him" (Jeremiah 36:4).

Whether you believe the stories in the Bible are real or made up, whether you believe they were written down right away or compiled much later, whether you believe the writers relied on great memories or reliable records or both, the message of the Bible—and the making of the Bible—are rooted in story. Good stories get told repeatedly, and the best stories almost always make their way into print.

This is true even in our time. You go to lunch with an old college pal who has a knack for getting into odd situations. Your friend, who is an engaging storyteller, proceeds to tell you about a bizarre weekend camping trip that included a flash flood, a runaway Shetland pony, and two Elvis impersonators. You are amused and amazed. Back at work, what do you do? You know exactly what you do. During a break, you turn to your colleague and say, "Okay, listen to the crazy story I heard at lunch . . ." Maybe you even write up the account and e-mail it to a few others. Perhaps you share it on Facebook.

This is exactly what the ancients did—in the days before cubicles and social media. Memorable stories were repeated orally around campfires and at tribal gatherings. They were learned by heart and passed on to children and grandchildren while hunting, preparing food, or getting ready for bed. At some point, especially noteworthy stories were written down—not on the Internet, of course, but using ancient writing materials. By the time of the Greeks, they were even put into long prose form and recounted from memory in huge amphitheaters.

We don't know exactly *when* the biblical authors sat down to record Israel's religious history for posterity. But at certain points along the way, the spoken word became the written word. These inscribed words, like their oral ancestors, were then passed along. They were copied and recopied. Compared and corrected. Collected and organized. Translated from Hebrew into Greek, Aramaic, and other languages. Bound in book form and carried to obscure places—like to a monastery at the base of a mountain called Sinai. There they were read, then stored or hidden . . . until someone with bushy sideburns came looking for them centuries later.

In 1853, Dr. Tischendorf returned to Saint Catherine's, in hopes of obtaining the eighty-six leaves of the rare manuscript he had left behind on his first trip. This time, the monks, suspicious of Tischendorf's not-so-veiled desire to remove documents from their monastery, were not as generous. He left with only a leather fragment of Genesis that he claimed was being used as a bookmark.

Ancient peoples wrote on all sorts of surfaces: wet clay, stone, bone, metals, and pottery (the shards of which are called *ostraca*).[3] For the biblical writers, the preferred materials were parchment and papyrus.

Many people think of *parchment* as brownish-colored paper that appears old and wrinkly, like the material on which replicas of America's Declaration of Independence are printed. In the world of ancient documents, however, parchment is animal skin—the hides of sheep, goats, cattle, even antelope—stretched thin, dried, and then cut like paper. (Although there were different ways of processing skins, we are using the term *parchment* here to refer to animal skin prepared for writing.) The highest quality parchments are referred to as *vellum*.

Parchment, as you might imagine, was expensive to produce. A large codex such as Sinaiticus would require the skins of perhaps two hundred animals! For this reason, some parchments were reused. The old ink was scraped off, and new information was written on the leathery surface (such a recycled parchment is referred to as a *palimpsest*). Because of its durable nature, parchment was popular until the late Middle Ages. That's when the Chinese introduced a paper made of cotton or hemp.

Papyrus is the other primary writing material of ancient documents. It was made from a tall, marshy plant that grew in delta regions such as the Nile. The plant's stems were cut open, sliced into strips, then placed side by side. A second layer of strips was laid at right angles to the first. When pressed tightly together and dried, the result was a usable kind of paper.

For writing on these various materials, reed pens were preferred. Ink was typically brown or black in color, and it was made from a solution of soot and gum or resin.

What about size? Our modern books are usually compact and easy to carry. With an e-reader, you can carry a thousand or more books with you at all times! Contemporary books also come with a table of contents, page numbers, and often an index.

Ancient biblical works possessed none of these features. Those written on parchment took the form of bulky scrolls, rolled up on sticks. With no chapter or verse divisions (those innovations didn't come about until the 1200s and 1500s, respectively), and with some scrolls being more than thirty feet in length, locating a specific passage proved to be a constant challenge, even though carefully placed spaces were used to divide paragraphs. What's more, all that unrolling and rerolling meant great wear and tear on the parchment.

Around the end of the first century CE, a different and more durable kind of document came into vogue—the *codex*. Codices (plural) closely resemble our modern books. They had leaves (pages) that were made of sheets of papyrus or parchment that had been folded and then stitched together. This format, unlike the scroll format, allowed for writing on both sides of the page, thus conserving space and saving on production expenses. It also meant that separate writings could be collected and bound together.

In February 1859—perhaps thinking, *The third time's a charm*—everyone's favorite German codex collector was back at Saint Catherine's. Pictures reveal Constantin von Tischendorf to be a plump man, possessing either a large forehead or quite a bit less hair, depending on your point of view. He was funded on this particular trip by none other than Alexander II, tsar of Russia.

Remembering the failure of his previous visit to Sinai, Tischendorf went out of his way to avoid discussing manuscripts with the monks. On the final night of his stay, he reportedly gave the monastery steward a gift: a recently published copy of the Septuagint. The steward responded to this gesture by saying, "I, too, have a

Septuagint." Taking Tischendorf to his chamber, the man retrieved a bundle wrapped in red cloth. Inside the cloth lay the rest of the 1,500-year-old manuscript Tischendorf had been dreaming about for fifteen years.

As nonchalantly as possible, Tischendorf asked if he might spend the evening looking over the ancient book. Granted this privilege, the scholar stayed up all night reading, studying, and making notes from the codex's 347 leaves. He later wrote about the experience in his diary, "It really seemed a sacrilege to sleep."[4]

The codex contained the entire New Testament (regarded as the oldest complete copy in existence) and about half of the Old. It also included the complete Apocrypha (the extra books that some, but not all, people of faith accept as inspired Scripture). What's more, it contained two additional extrabiblical works from the second century—much of the Shepherd of Hermas, and all of the Epistle of Barnabas. It didn't take long for Tischendorf to conclude that this book was "the most precious Biblical treasure in existence."[5]

The day of his departure, Tischendorf offered to buy the manuscript from Saint Catherine's. The monk in charge would not sell it. Could he take it to the monastery's extension in Cairo to study it? Again, the eager scholar was rebuffed.

According to which source you read, the details vary regarding what happened next. The most circulated version of events says that Tischendorf prevailed upon the abbot of Saint Catherine's in Cairo to send for the manuscript. From March to May he was allowed to examine the codex eight leaves at a time. With the help of two German associates who knew some Greek, Tischendorf transcribed the entire document.

As the scholar continued his travels in the Middle East, he couldn't get the codex off his mind. In September, Tischendorf returned to Cairo and worked out a deal to borrow the ancient book. Promising to return it safely to the monastery, he was allowed to take it to St. Petersburg, Russia, and compare it to his recent transcription. This is where everything got weird.

What the monastery thought was a strict loan agreement, Tischendorf apparently saw as a loan with an option to donate. All along he had been pressuring the monastery to part with the codex, to bequeath it to the tsar. (He had learned that it was time to select a new abbot for the monks at Saint Catherine's. Perhaps he argued, the tsar—as the civil protector of the Greek Orthodox Church, and one with influence in such matters—might be persuaded to appoint the abbot of the monks' choosing, in exchange for their gift of this old Greek manuscript?)

The entire arrangement became a giant, messy misunderstanding. But all the back-and-forth claims aside, these facts remain: Tischendorf got his precious codex, and he eventually published a facsimile edition at Leipzig. Then, after the codex sat for seven years in St. Petersburg, it was "donated" in 1869 to the tsar by the Greek Orthodox Archbishop of Sinai on behalf of the Sinai monks. It never returned to Saint Catherine's.

In exchange for this priceless artifact, the monastery received 9,000 rubles, a silver shrine, and the appointment of their candidate as abbot.

Four years later Constantin von Tischendorf died at age fifty-nine, reportedly from overwork and exhaustion. In 2015, on the occasion of his two hundredth birthday, some hailed Tischendorf as a hero. Others remembered him as a scoundrel.[6]

The story of Codex Sinaiticus doesn't end with the death of Dr. Tischendorf. Following the Russian Revolution, Joseph Stalin's government, hungry for cash, sold the 347 leaves of this ancient codex to the British Museum for what was then the equivalent of half a million dollars. The codex arrived the day after Christmas in 1933. To this day, tourists to London can see this priceless treasure with their own eyes.

In May 1975, while officials at Saint Catherine's were cleaning out a room under Saint George's Chapel, they came across a stack of old documents and manuscript fragments. In this cache of papers were eighteen more pages (or page fragments) of the 1,500-year-old codex!

Thanks to Constantin von Tischendorf's three visits to the base of Mount Sinai, 414 of Codex Sinaiticus' leaves (estimated to originally number about 740) have been preserved. Today, these parchments live in four different places: the British Museum (347 leaves), the Leipzig University Library (43 leaves), the National Library of Russia (portions of 6 leaves), and the 18 leaves found in 1975 and remaining at Saint Catherine's. Among the missing pages? All five books of the Pentateuch—the books that tell the beginning of Israel's story and the related story of how at Sinai, the world began to get the remarkable book we call the Bible.

It is thanks to another man, who lived some 3,100 years before Tischendorf and who, according to the biblical narrative, made multiple trips up and down Mount Sinai (Exodus 19:3, 8, 20; 20:1–19, 21; 24:9, 11, 12; 32:1–4, 31; 34:2), that we have those remarkable details. According to Judeo-Christian tradition, Moses's famous stone tablets, together with the other writings God told him to undertake, are the beginning of the Bible. The Bible records that this book of the covenant was placed in something called the "ark of the covenant," and then Moses and the Israelites departed Sinai (Numbers 10:12).

CHAPTER TWO

PEOPLE OF THE BOOK

THE PROPHETS AND THE WRITINGS

What difference does it make if Moses wrote it or if some other prophet wrote it, since all of their words are true and divinely inspired?!

—RABBI JOSEPH BONFILS, FOURTEENTH-CENTURY TALMUDIST AND BIBLE COMMENTATOR

Remember several years ago when people around the world were holding their breath because the Nazis had located the Jewish ark of the covenant and were on the verge of using it for their evil purposes?

Actually, that's a description of millions of popcorn-eating, nail-biting moviegoers while watching the 1981 blockbuster hit *Raiders of the Lost Ark.*

Since almost everyone has seen this thrill-a-minute film, it's no spoiler to recount that the Nazis were thwarted by heroic archaeologist Indiana Jones and by the supernatural power of the ark itself. Just before the credits rolled, we watched this ancient, enigmatic container get boxed up in a crate marked "Top Secret" . . . then stored in a massive, shadowy government warehouse.

Steven Spielberg's Oscar-winning movie raises a serious question (even if it doesn't attempt to give a serious answer): What happened to the mysterious golden box of the Jewish people?

Scripture describes the ark of the covenant as a container made of acacia wood and overlaid with gold (Exodus 25:10–22). It says the ark contained a jar of manna—the heavenly bread that God supplied for the Israelites after they left Egypt (Exodus 16:33)—and the rod of Aaron (Moses's brother and Israel's first high priest), which had miraculously budded (Numbers 17:8; Hebrews 9:4).

Most importantly, the ark is said to have contained the law of God, engraved on stone tablets that Moses received on Mount Sinai (Exodus 25:16; Hebrews 9:4). We know that this weighty (literally) divine agreement was the ark's most significant item, if for no other reason than the box is referred to as the ark *of the covenant.*

For hundreds of years, this relic-filled chest was central to Jewish worship. The ark was housed first in the tabernacle (Israel's portable worship tent). Later it found a home in Solomon's Temple in Jerusalem. Around the time the Babylonians conquered

Jerusalem in 586 BCE, the ark and its contents vanished. Some speculate the chest was destroyed when the temple got demolished. Others suggest the ark was taken into captivity with the Jewish people—and eventually lost.

But there are plenty of other theories that the ark was smuggled out of the temple, perhaps even out of the country, and hidden. There are wild allegations that the Knights Templar, a papal military order active in the twelfth century, found the ark and took it various places, including to Oak Island off the coast of Canada. The best-selling thriller *The Da Vinci Code* accented these fantastic but fictitious claims.[1]

The most enduring claim comes from Christians in Ethiopia. They insist the ark and its contents are in their possession, in a heavily guarded chapel in the remote city of Aksum. They further claim they have had it for *three millennia*! According to their version of events, Menelik (a son born to the queen of Sheba—and allegedly fathered by Israel's King Solomon) visited his dad at age twenty. When he returned home from Jerusalem, the story goes, his entourage smuggled the ark back to Africa. For anyone who likes conspiracy theories, this story is enough to get the heart racing. However, it is worth noting that not even the leaders of the Ethiopian church have ever been allowed to see the ark or its contents. That honor is reserved for a few nameless monks and priests who serve as caretakers of the ark.

It is a fantastic claim—the religious equivalent of Bigfoot sightings. If we could gain access to the Church of Saint Mary of Zion—the little chapel behind the big iron fence in northern

Ethiopia—what are the odds that we would see an actual golden chest with sculpted angels stretching their golden wings over its cover? If by some impossible chance the ark of the covenant *were* there, and if we peeked inside—assuming our faces didn't melt off as in Spielberg's movie—would we actually see Moses's stone tablets and maybe also some other ancient writings?

This is what we know for sure: the Bible records that when the Israelites traveled to the land promised to Abraham and his descendants, they were led by priests from the tribe of Levi. Some of those men carried a mysterious, ornate box that contained the tablets of the Ten Commandments (Numbers 10:33).

It's no wonder that some have described the Israelites as "the people of the book." They were governed and guided by words they regarded as holy.

As previously mentioned, the traditional view is that between the Israelites' departure from Sinai and their entrance into Canaan, Moses composed the entire Pentateuch (except, of course, for the final part of Deuteronomy that describes his death). The more modern, critical view held by many academics is that these books were written much later in Israel's history. (That's a complicated debate for another time . . . and a much thicker book.)

Either way, the point is that the Bible was a work in progress. It remained under construction for a very long time. Paul McCartney of Beatles fame claims he woke up one day and the mega-hit song

"Yesterday" was in his head. Grabbing a notepad, he scribbled down the lyrics in *less than a minute*. Just like that—song complete.

The process of writing the Hebrew Bible wasn't nearly that quick or painless.

After the death of Moses, the Israelites are said to have followed the ark of the covenant and a military commander named Joshua into Canaan. In the biblical book that bears his name, Joshua leads the Israelites to victory over most of the land's inhabitants. We also see him reading the law of Moses to the people (Joshua 8:30–35) and exhorting them "to observe the commandment and instruction that Moses the servant of the Lord commanded you" (Joshua 22:5).

The question naturally arises: Did Joshua write the book that is named after him? Well, he wrote *something*. Just before his death, he led the Jewish people in a covenant renewal ceremony, after which the Bible says he "wrote these words in the book of the law of God" (Joshua 24:26).

After Joshua's death, the Israelites wearied of war. They decided to coexist with the remaining inhabitants of Canaan. The book of Judges (composed by an unknown author) describes a period marked by spiritual decline, foreign oppression, and social anarchy. During this era, the ark of the covenant containing the book of the law moved to Bethel (Judges 20:26–27). Later it found a home in Shiloh (1 Samuel 4:3). Though it was briefly captured by the

Philistines, it was eagerly returned when its captors were stricken by a severe plague (1 Samuel 5).

About this time (ca. 1000 BCE) the Israelites began clamoring for a king. Before anointing Saul as Israel's first monarch, the prophet Samuel is described as writing *something* in a book and laying it before the Lord (1 Samuel 10:25).

Here's what we can conclude from this history: if the book revered by "the people of the book" wasn't yet officially being written in earnest, the stories that would one day comprise it were being diligently collected and preserved.

Following King Saul, until about 930 BCE, two more kings reigned in succession over Israel: David and his son Solomon. A sizable portion of the Tanakh (the Hebrew Bible, or Old Testament) documents this period. The books of 1 and 2 Samuel describe the turbulent reigns of Saul and David. First Chronicles adds a priestly perspective on David's rule. Almost half the Psalms are attributed to David.

An important note: for the longest time, many scholars remained dubious of David. Since there was no evidence beyond the Bible for either his life or his kingship, many historians put David in the category of King Arthur. Or, they concluded, if he existed at all, he was a local chieftain, not the leader of a large nation. But in 1993, while digging at Tel Dan in northern Israel, archaeologist Avraham Biran found a *stela*—a stone slab—with an Aramean inscription that referred to a "king of the House of David." This marker, erected by one of Israel's fiercest enemies and dated to the ninth century BCE (a century or so after David's death), is seen as conclusive evidence of a real-life King David and a royal dynasty.

The reign of David's son Solomon is depicted in 1 Kings and 2 Chronicles. This was Israel's golden era—a time of peace, prominence, and prosperity. Solomon's greatest achievement was the construction of the temple in Jerusalem.

The ark of the covenant occupied the most sacred, central part of this magnificent structure—called the *holy of holies*. Traditionally, several of the Bible's "Writings" (*Ketuvim*, as they are known by Jewish readers) have been viewed as Solomon's works: the books of Proverbs, Ecclesiastes, and Song of Songs, plus a couple of the psalms.

Solomon is universally renowned for his wisdom. Students of history, however, note his foolish policies of excessive taxation and conscripting citizens into royal service. In the short term, this system of corvée (forced, unpaid) labor turned Jerusalem into a showplace. In the long term, it filled the people with resentment.

After Solomon's death, the nation split into two kingdoms (1 Kings 12). The ten northern tribes became known as Israel. The two tribes in the south took the name Judah. Each kingdom had a long series of kings and experienced a prolonged, perceptible decline. The biblical accounts of this divided kingdom era (1 Kings 12–2 Kings 25; 2 Chronicles 10–36) show the people of the book gradually straying from the instructions and commands of the book.

Enter the prophets—men like Isaiah and Jeremiah, Hosea and Amos—who implored the two nations to return to their spiritual roots. (The biblical documents bearing these prophets' names comprise the bulk of the second section of the Hebrew Bible and the final seventeen books of the Christian Old Testament.) Except for a few short-lived revivals in the Southern Kingdom under a few spiritually minded kings, the Bible shows that many of the Israelites spurned these prophetic warnings.

One of the most intriguing stories from this era happened during the reign of King Josiah (2 Kings 22–23). According to the biblical account, Josiah, the grandson of the evil King Manasseh and son of the wicked King Amon, ascended to the throne when he was only eight years old. Eighteen years into his reign, Josiah called for a major renovation of the temple. It was at the start of this process that Hilkiah, the high priest, announced, "I have found the book of the law in the house of the LORD" (2 Kings 22:8). Although many Bible scholars see this narrative as reflecting the initial publication of the book of Deuteronomy, the Bible maintains that this book existed from the time of Moses, thus emphasizing the tremendous loss of continuity of the biblical text that seems to have occurred.

Picking up the Bible's account again, when the royal secretary read the words of the divine covenant to Josiah, the young monarch was overcome. He ripped his clothes—a sign of mourning, repentance, and humility. Then he called for sweeping religious reforms in the nation. He led the people of Judah in a lavish celebration of Passover, as it hadn't been observed since the time of the Judges. This was remarkable—even more so because many citizens of the rival Northern Kingdom traveled south and participated! As long as Josiah lived, he attempted to govern Judah by the book.

The story is told of a young Jewish man who inquired of a wise old rabbi, "Why does the Torah tell us to put God's commandments *on* our hearts? Wouldn't we be better off to hide the holy words *in* our hearts?" The sage thought for a moment and said, "Moses commanded us to put the sacred words *on* our hearts, so that when dark times come and our hearts break apart, God's truth can fall *in*."

The Jewish people soon faced such dark, heartbreaking times. In 722 BCE, the Northern Kingdom was decimated by Assyria, and many Israelites were exiled to Assyria and farther east. In 597 BCE, the Babylonians laid siege to Jerusalem and the Southern Kingdom, eventually pillaging the temple and carrying many Jewish citizens into captivity. In 586 BCE, a second siege by the Babylonians ended in the deportation of thousands more Jews, as well as the complete destruction of Jerusalem and the temple. Thus ended what is known as the First Temple period (ca. 1006–586 BCE).

Scholars can't seem to agree on which biblical writings the exiled Jews took with them into Babylonian captivity. How much of the Bible was already written? What books were composed during this national "time-out"?

Traditionalists tend to date most of the Old Testament writings early. For example, you can find Bible teachers who believe Moses authored the Torah as early as 1405 BCE. Some claim Solomon authored Proverbs, Ecclesiastes, and Song of Solomon in the tenth century BCE. If they are correct, the exiled Israelites would have had much Scripture to fortify them during this bleak period.

But many modern scholars are convinced that the bulk of the Hebrew Bible was composed *during* and *after* this time of exile. They see this trilogy of disasters—the fall of Jerusalem, the destruction of the temple, and the dispersion of the Jewish people—as the primary catalysts for a concerted effort to preserve the nation's religious history via the written word.

The questions behind most of the biblical books—"Who wrote this?" and "When was it written?"—are hotly debated. But make no mistake: all during the First Temple period, events *were* being documented. Records *were* being kept. The Bible references other books that were written to preserve for posterity Israel's social, political, and religious history. These writings are not regarded as Scripture, but they served as background for the writing of Scripture. Note the various sources mentioned in these Bible verses (emphasis added):

- "Wherefore it is said in the *Book of the Wars* of the LORD . . ." (Numbers 21:14).
- "(He ordered that The Song of the Bow be taught to the people of Judah; it is written in the *Book of Jashar*)" (2 Samuel 1:18).

- "Now the rest of the acts of Solomon, all that he did as well as his wisdom, are they not written in the *Book of the Acts of Solomon*?" (1 Kings 11:41).
- "Now the rest of the acts of Jeroboam, how he warred and how he reigned, are written in the *Book of the Annals of the Kings of Israel*" (1 Kings 14:19).
- "Now the rest of the acts of Rehoboam, and all that he did, are they not written in the *Book of the Annals of the Kings of Judah*?" (1 Kings 14:29).
- "So all Israel was enrolled by genealogies; and these are written in the *Book of the Kings of Israel*" (1 Chronicles 9:1).
- "The acts of Asa, from first to last, are written in the *Book of the Kings of Judah and Israel*" (2 Chronicles 16:11).
- "Accounts of his sons, and of the many oracles against him, and of the rebuilding of the house of God are written in the *Commentary on the Book of the Kings*" (2 Chronicles 24:27).

The implications are clear: whatever portions of the Bible may have been written during the Babylonian exile to encourage a scattered, disheartened people, the writers had a whole library of source material to pull from. Unfortunately these books mentioned as sources in the Bible are no longer in existence.

The people of the book wrote that book with the help of other books.

Thanks to about 200 cuneiform tablets, we know that there were Jewish exiles in Babylon—and we know something about their business affairs. Called the Al-Yahudu Archive, these ancient clay records are written in Akkadian and date from as early as 570 BCE. Among other things, they include tax records and land lease agreements.

We do not, however, know many details about the religious lives of the Jews who were exiled to Babylon in the sixth century BCE. From the Al-Yahudu tablets, we do know that Jews settled together and maintained their culture. They didn't have a temple in which to worship and offer sacrifices. Nevertheless, they gathered to study the law of God and pray. Their religious leaders worked to keep the nation's spiritual heritage alive.

After the Persian king Cyrus overthrew the Babylonians in 539 BCE, he issued an unexpected decree: the captive Jews were free to return to their homeland.

Not everyone took advantage of this offer. Many Jews remained in Babylon (their life-and-death story is told in the book of Esther). Those who returned to Judea did so in three big waves. The first group was led by Zerubbabel and focused on rebuilding the temple. Next came the group led by Ezra the priest, who moved to Jerusalem with a mission to teach God's Word to the returnees. A final group was led by Nehemiah. A government official, Nehemiah relocated for the express purpose of rebuilding the city's walls and restoring Jerusalem's economic and religious role. Despite fierce opposition and a less-than-experienced workforce, this massive project was accomplished in less than two months!

This postexilic era—also called the Second Temple period—is described in the biblical books of Ezra and Nehemiah. The prophetic writings named after Haggai, Zechariah, and Malachi provide a spiritual perspective.

During this time, the land of Judah was a giant construction zone. The temple, private homes, businesses, the walls of the City of David—in every direction things were being built or rebuilt.

Meanwhile, another group was hard at work on something else: the book. The spiritual library of the Jewish people—Israel's national scrapbook—was under construction too.

The rebuilding of the temple in Jerusalem necessitated the re-formation and re-emergence of religious professionals. Who else but devoted priests and teachers could help the Israelites return to their divine calling to be "the people of the book"?

There was much to be done. The sacred scrolls that had been carried to and from Babylon were in bad shape—dog-eared from study and crumbling from the wear and tear of travel. Newer writings had been produced during the exile. Prophets were still speaking and writing. Perhaps some residents of the land brought to the rededicated temple ancient scrolls that had remained hidden in Judah during the exile.

We are left with a thousand questions: Where were these biblical writings kept? How soon did the nation's religious leaders set up scriptoria—special rooms for writing and copying documents?

And what about the original writings—such as Moses's stone tablets, the psalms ascribed to King David, or those mystery documents the Bible says Joshua and Samuel wrote? Were any of those still around in 500 BCE? Is there any chance they are still around today?

Don't you wish an archaeologist would uncover these items at an excavation site this week? Can you imagine getting to see such things on display at a world-class museum—the Shrine of the Book in Jerusalem, the British Library in London, or the Museum of the Bible in Washington, DC?

The answer, which may shock you, is this: we will never see any of those original writings.

Documents—even very important ones—deteriorate. They are inherently fragile, which makes preserving them critical.

Take the Declaration of Independence as one example. Historians tell us that someone spilled water on it while trying to copy it back in the early 1820s. Years later, a government official had the bright idea (pun intended) of tacking it up on a sunlit wall in the US Patent Office. There, this vital piece of American history hung for decades, until someone commented that it appeared to be fading. Despite this warning, it wasn't until after the document turned 175 that attempts at preserving it became serious.

In the early 1950s, the Declaration was placed in a bronze, helium-filled case in the dimly lit National Archives building.

There it lay for years under special glass designed to filter out harmful light and fend off bullets. In 2003, scientists decided those measures weren't good enough. They gave America's charter of liberty a newer and stronger titanium case, filled with inert argon gas. Tonight, just as every night, this case and its precious contents will descend twenty-two feet into a reinforced steel and concrete vault.

All this newfangled, around-the-clock protection, and yet, if you have ever seen this history-changing document, you know how faint and worn it is. And it's not yet 250 years old.[2]

In a world of fires and floods, a world where sometimes even well-meaning people are careless, the owner of a precious document can't be too careful. This is why we do our best to protect our important papers. We duplicate vital records. We make certified hard copies or digitized electronic copies. We store those copies in filing cabinets or safety deposit boxes, on computer hard drives or in the cloud.

The ancient Jews faced the same dilemma. Extensive handling and study over a long time caused their valuable scrolls to become tattered and torn. Consequently, before they became illegible, these fading, crumbling documents were reproduced with the utmost care.

The Talmud speaks of burying holy books that had become unusable. By the Middle Ages, deteriorating writings were stored in special repositories called *genizahs*. Eventually, the Jews developed the practice whereby at a chosen time, they would take these old scrolls and parchments from the genizah and bury them in a solemn ceremony.

If scientific estimates are accurate—that a plastic bottle buried in a landfill today will decompose completely in 1,000 years and that an aluminum soda can will disintegrate in 200 years, how long do you think papyrus and parchment last under the earth?

Now do you see why we don't have any of the original writings (also known as *autographs*) of the Bible? The documents that weren't accidentally lost or destroyed may have been intentionally buried!

Wise observers of human nature have observed that the loss of these autographs might be a blessing in disguise. If we had any actual documents handwritten by Moses or David, those artifacts wouldn't be up for auction at Sotheby's. They'd likely be objects of worship.

So, we don't have any of the original biblical documents. But we do have copies—lots and lots of copies.

Who did all this writing and copying of documents in ancient Israel? The *scribes*. The word in Hebrew is *soferim*, which means "people who can write." It probably comes from a verb that means "to write or inscribe," derived from a noun meaning "document." In short, the scribes were a group of people—oftentimes from the same extended family (1 Chronicles 2:55)—with the ability to read and write, in an era when not everyone could. Their charge was to record accurately and to meticulously transcribe information—much, but not all, of which was religious in nature (1 Kings 4:3; 2 Kings 18:18; 1 Chronicles 27:32).

When making sacred copies of Scripture, especially for use in public worship, scribes followed strict rules to ensure accurate reproductions of the Torah. They had to immerse in a ritual bath, known as a *mikveh*, and be clothed respectfully for this holy task. Nothing made of iron or steel could be used, since those materials were used to make weapons.

Scribes used reeds sharpened into the shape of pens and wrote only on the skins of kosher animals. Letters had to conform to a certain size and style and could not touch. During the medieval period, the famous Jewish sage Maimonides recommended that the columns on each page be from forty-eight to sixty lines in length and be uniform throughout the scroll. The ink could only be black and made by a special recipe. Nothing, not even the smallest letter, could be written from memory. Full concentration while copying was mandated. It is said that if a king were to address a scribe while he was writing the name of God, the king was to be ignored until the writer finished his work. If a Torah scroll was found to have a single mistake or even one missing letter (out of its required 304,805 letters), it was not to be used in worship.

During the Babylonian exile and afterward (during the Second Temple period, 516 BCE to 70 CE), a second kind of scribe emerged. These weren't merely competent secretaries and copyists but men learned in the Torah. They attended scribal schools (an ancient version of a Bible college, yeshiva, or divinity school) where they sat under the teaching of scholars such as Ezra (Ezra 7:10–11).

Scribes during this period were esteemed for their knowledge of the written Jewish law and trained to interpret and proclaim these truths to the people. They were the continuators of the tradition of the Jewish prophets, the founders of the oral law, and the forerunners of modern rabbis. Though these later scribes may have copied documents on occasion, this was not a large part of their regular job description.

From stone tablets at Sinai to scrolls in Babylon to parchments in Palestine, the spiritual history of the Hebrew people gradually found its way into writing. When the Jews at last returned to their homeland in the Persian period (after 540 BCE), the stage was finally set for this community of faith with its curious collection of religious writings to fulfill their destiny as the people of the book.

CHAPTER THREE

THE TIMES THEY ARE A-CHANGIN'

Between the Testaments

In Jewish history there are no coincidences.

—Elie Wiesel, Holocaust survivor,

Nobel Prize winner, and author, *Night*

His skin may have been old and wrinkled, but his memory was clear.

The incident had happened, he said, when he was much younger. Perhaps the 1920s, but he couldn't be sure because when a person lives a nomadic life, the months and years tend to run together.

He recalled that his Tamireh tribe was doing what bedouin peoples have done for centuries: wandering the desert regions south and east of Jerusalem. Searching out any patches of grass for the flocks to nibble. Making the rounds of all the known springs. On this day, his tent was not far from the northwestern edge of the Dead Sea.

His stomach ached from emptiness—he remembered that. Even more so when he startled a sand partridge, causing it to fly up suddenly from behind a rock. Instantly the hungry herdsman turned hunter. He stalked the bird through a wadi and watched it pause on a ledge. Then, just as it began to fly, he took aim and fired.

A perfect shot. Only the partridge didn't drop. To his surprise, it took off, a pinwheel of feathers and wings. The bird ricocheted off one rock, fell onto another, then flap-hopped along a ledge on the cliff. The old man paused, smiled, and shook his head as he told how the wounded bird disappeared into a small opening on the rock face.

Being a young man, and being ravenous, he wasn't about to let a little bit of climbing deter him from a much-needed meal. Up the cliff he went.

It took some effort, but when he reached eye level with the hole, he found it larger than he had expected. It opened into a good-sized cave. Pulling himself up and into the cool darkness, he let his eyes adjust to the light. He located his bird—and something more.

The floor of the cave was covered with broken pottery. Among the shards, he noticed a very old oil lamp. He examined it and found it to be in good condition. Tucking the lamp into his garments, he felt his stomach rumble. He grabbed his prey and scrambled out of the cave back into the desert sun.

After roasting and eating the partridge, and then giving the lamp to his mother, the man said he didn't think again about the bird, the cave, or the pottery for decades. Not until that very night, when sitting by a campfire, he listened to some younger bedouin men talking about all the things people were finding in nearby caves.

Who put pottery in a remote cliffside cave near Qumran? When did this happen and why? What is the ancient history behind what archaeologists call the Cave of the Wounded Partridge?

To answer these questions, we have to go back in time—long before the 1920s. Let's travel all the way back to 538 BCE.

Imagine, for a moment, being an exiled Israelite, in Babylon, in the sixth century BCE.

Unless you have an unusually large number of candles on your birthday cake, life in Babylon is all you've ever known. Stories about the holy city of Jerusalem and Solomon's glorious temple are just that—handed-down stories, not personal memories.

Thanks to your parents and grandparents, you know all about Abraham, Moses, and King David. You've heard of the golden ark of the covenant that—at least at one time—contained stone tablets said to be inscribed by God himself.

You know by heart many of the old songs of Zion—many of which are ascribed to David. Each Sabbath you gather with family members and Jewish neighbors to practice your faith. It's a bittersweet experience. There's no temple, so you turn west and pray toward Jerusalem, where the temple used to be. You listen as some priest or scribe or prophet in the community opens the sacred scrolls and explains why and how you should live by the ancient law of God. It bugs you that you can't read Hebrew as well as your parents did. It worries you deeply that your children don't read it at all.

In 538 BCE, a new king takes control: Cyrus, the ruler of the Persian Empire. He issues a shocking decree that, after more than half a century in captivity, the Jewish people will be permitted to return to the beloved homeland most have never seen. Though most of your friends decide to remain in Babylon, you and your family excitedly return to Judea.

What you find is heartbreaking, a punch in the gut. It's worse than you heard. You arrive to find a city—and a people—in need of an extreme makeover.

As far as the creation of the Hebrew Bible (the Christian Old Testament) is concerned, no block of time is more significant than the postexilic era or the Second Temple period (roughly the five centuries leading up to the Common Era). Some Christians refer to part of this time—the years between the close of Old Testament history and the beginning of New Testament history—as the "silent" years. They were anything but.

This is the time when Israel endured domination by a series of foreign powers and thereby grappled with its social-political-religious identity. This is the era when the last of the books of the Hebrew Bible were composed. It's also when the twenty-four Hebrew books (the same books that make up the Old Testament of the Christian Bible, only in a different order) were being gathered into a widely accepted canon of Scripture.

Canon comes from a Greek word that means "standard," "reed," or "measuring stick." When speaking of Bible books as *canonical*, we mean they are part of the accepted list of writings that measure up to the standard of being inspired. Rather than a subjective title that people arbitrarily bestow on a work, *canonicity* is a formal, holy quality that a consensus of people recognizes in a particular writing. *Canonization* is the process of acknowledging, then treating as holy, a certain work. The *canon* is what you have when you bring all those sacrosanct writings together.

Historians typically divide the pivotal years leading up to the Common Era according to which empire was dominating the world stage. Thus, we hear about the Persian period (538–333 BCE), the Hellenistic or Greek period (333–63 BCE), and the Roman period (63 BCE–313 CE). Let's briefly examine key developments during each of these periods.

Beginning about 538 BCE, some Israelites, by decree of King Cyrus, left Babylon for their homeland. Others elected to stay. Still others began relocating to other parts of the Mediterranean, as well as to Persia, Syria, and North Africa. One fifth-century BCE example of this *diaspora* (dispersion or scattering) is the group of Jews who formed a colony and built a small temple on Elephantine Island in Egypt.

Historians usually give the starting point of the Hellenistic (or Greek) period as 333 BCE, though Hellenism itself had already begun to spread widely. However, it was in this year that a brash Macedonian king confronted and conquered the mighty Persian Empire. We know this brilliant leader—tutored by Aristotle and not yet twenty-five years old—as Alexander the Great. He is worthy of his nickname due to his great ambition to bring all people everywhere under Greek influence.

In defeating Persia, Alexander acquired Palestine. This is how all things Greek—language, cultural practices, philosophical ideas—began to infiltrate Jewish thought and life.

Alexander died suddenly in 323 BCE. Historians don't know if he was poisoned or if he contracted a disease like meningitis or West Nile virus. They do know that, since Alexander died without an heir, his top generals divvied up the Greek Empire. Ptolemy established a dynasty based in Egypt and had jurisdiction over Palestine. Seleucus took control of the eastern empire (Syria and Babylonia). Under this arrangement, the Jews living in and around Jerusalem (Judea) were allowed a fair amount of autonomy for more than a century.

However, within Judaism there was a fierce debate over the extent to which the Jewish people should assimilate into Hellenistic culture. By 198 BCE, the Seleucid ruler Antiochus III was in control of Palestine. Further attempts at Hellenization caused growing unrest. By 175 BCE, Antiochus IV Epiphanes, the son of Antiochus III, had assumed the throne. The Jewish debate escalated into civil strife. To support the Jewish Hellenists, Epiphanes moved to prohibit Jewish practices that he felt were adding to the cultural tension. He outlawed the ritual of circumcision. He ordered the destruction of Torah scrolls and made the possession of Hebrew Scriptures a capital offense. He erected an idol of Zeus at the temple and commanded the Jews to worship it. Finally, he committed the ultimate abomination: he sacrificed a pig on the temple's sacred altar.

These outrageous acts likely contributed to Epiphanes earning the nickname Epimanes ("the Mad One"). They definitely triggered a revolt. Led by the family of Judas Maccabeus, the Jews launched a guerilla campaign against the Seleucids beginning in 168 BCE. This war culminated with a Jewish victory and the rededication of the temple in 164 BCE. (It would take two more decades before the last occupants of the Seleucid fortress in Jerusalem would be expelled, giving the Jews complete independence.)

The Jewish feast of Hanukkah ("dedication") celebrates the victory over Antiochus and the Seleucids. Moreover, the holiday celebrates the purification and rededication of the Jerusalem temple. Rabbinical tradition says that, following their victory, the Maccabees had only enough oil to light the temple Menorah (a large golden candelabra with seven lamps) for one day. Nevertheless, the Menorah continued to burn for eight days! Though some question the veracity of the story about the Menorah, the basic events leading to the revolt and the regaining of Jewish independence are seen by Jewish tradition and modern historians as factual. Each December the story is retold with joy.

These events ushered in what historians call the Hasmonean dynasty. In the initial years after the revolt, the brothers of Judas Maccabeus preserved this shaky Jewish independence and promoted traditional Jewish culture and religious belief. But subsequent Hasmonean rulers, and the upper classes associated with them, were influenced by Greek ideas and were unwilling or unable to slow the gradual Hellenization of Judea.

In 63 BCE, the Roman general Pompey marched his troops into Palestine. Like a wounded partridge darting into a cave, the Jews retreated behind the walls of Jerusalem. Ever the relentless hunter, Pompey watched and waited. When his patience wore out, he broke into the city, barged into the temple, and slaughtered the priests on duty.

Just like that, Palestine was occupied again. This new Roman period would last from 63 BCE to 313 CE.

Now we are getting closer to why a bedouin herdsman in the 1920s found pottery shards in a cave near the Dead Sea. The answer lies in the tumultuous rise and fall of those three great empires—the Persians, the Greeks, and the Romans.

Not that life before this international game of "musical kingdoms" was predictable and peaceful, but postexilic Judaism was radically different. For the Jewish people, the final centuries leading up to the Common Era were marked by political turmoil and social upheaval. Everything kept shifting.

There were major geographic shifts. Prior to 725 BCE, if you were Jewish, you lived in the land of Israel, plain and simple. But beginning with the fall of the Northern Kingdom to Assyria in 722 BCE, and continuing through the Babylonian exile beginning in 597 BCE, more and more Jews lived outside Palestine. Many were forced to leave. Others left of their own accord (or refused to return when given the opportunity). This steady migration is alluded to in a claim in the Sibylline Oracles that "every land and sea was filled with the Jews."

The era brought significant religious shifts—enormous spiritual challenges first felt during the Babylonian exile. The Jews were hundreds of miles from home and immersed in a pagan culture. With a patchwork priesthood and no temple in which to offer sacrifices, the people were forced to improvise. Prayers were substituted for animal sacrifices. Reading the Torah replaced worshiping at the temple. Simpler, smaller local gatherings replaced ornate worship rituals in a large, lavish temple. After the exile, and especially as Jews migrated to foreign lands, this decentralized way of expressing the Jewish faith gave birth to the movement to build local synagogues.

There were also extreme cultural shifts. Centuries under foreign influence took their toll. By 250 BCE, a growing number of Jews—especially those living outside Palestine—could no longer speak Hebrew, much less read the Hebrew Bible. Greek had become the accepted international language of politics and commerce, much as English is today. Many devout Jews worried that their unique Hebrew way of life was dying, or at least being dangerously compromised by outside influences.

There were profound political shifts. By the second century BCE, several distinct sects had developed within Palestinian Judaism. The Sadducees were the aristocratic, politically connected party. Some tended to be Hellenized, but others were fiercely protective of the temple and the Torah, and they were vitally interested in maintaining the status quo.

The Pharisees were famous for advocating not only the written law but, just as importantly, the oral traditions that were later embodied in the *oral law* (interpretations of the written Torah by prominent scribes and rabbis). Though the Pharisees had little real political power, they were popular with the masses.

A third sect, the Essenes, were strict in their views on personal purity and zealous for national righteousness. These beliefs prompted them to want to separate themselves from a Jewish culture they perceived as corrupt and worldly. (This group may have left us the Dead Sea Scrolls.)

Given these enormous shifts, it's easy to see why the Jews of this postexilic era began grasping for something stable. The book had served as Israel's guide in difficult times in the past, so in Second Temple times the people of the book clung to it as well.

A flurry of significant biblical developments began to unfold. Led by scribes and prophets, the Jewish people during the Second Temple period continued recording their history, writing prophetic words, collecting and collating the wisdom of the ages written before and during the exile. They carefully assessed each writing. They studied and reproduced the manuscripts they deemed holy and useful. Once identified as such, they worked feverishly to translate, teach, and disseminate Scripture.

As time passed, more and more Jews embraced Greek language and culture. Fewer and fewer were able to read and understand the Hebrew Torah. By 250 BCE, there was a serious need (and a growing demand) for a Greek translation of the Scriptures. A famous, ancient letter—the Letter of Aristeas—tells the story.

The royal librarian in Alexandria, Egypt, approached the king of Egypt, Ptolemy II (282–246 BCE), asking for a Greek copy of the Pentateuch. The king, in turn, asked Eleazar, the high priest in Jerusalem, to assemble a crackerjack translation team. He did so, supposedly bringing six scholars from each of Israel's twelve tribes to Alexandria and ordering them to get to work.

Today, with computer software and online tools like Google Translate, it's possible to render an entire page of text in a different language almost instantly. But 2,300 years ago, such work was tedious and time-consuming.

Yet, as the story is told in the Letter of Aristeas and in a parallel account in the Babylonian Talmud, these seventy-two men completed this formidable task in just seventy-two days! The finished product was called the *Septuagint* (abbreviated as LXX), which is Latin for *seventy*. (It was rounded off to seventy perhaps because the Latin word for seventy-two, *septuaginta duo*, doesn't flow off the tongue as well.)

Over time, this story became grander and more eye-popping. Justin Martyr, a prominent Christian scholar and writer in the second century CE, claimed it wasn't just the Torah that the men translated in slightly more than ten weeks; it was the entire Hebrew Bible. Around 400 CE, the theologian Augustine chimed in, saying that even though each of the seventy-two translators had worked independently, they all ended up with the exact same wording! The Talmudic account asserted that all seventy-two had miraculously made the same intentional modifications to avoid translating literally passages that might be misleading or insulting to the Egyptians.

It's hard to know how much of this story is fact and how much is fiction. Most likely, the work was carried out in stages and continued into the late second century BCE. But however it happened, the end result was this: for Jews who no longer spoke or read Hebrew, the LXX made the message of the Bible come alive. And for the first time in history, non-Jews could also read and study the law of God.

Copies of the Septuagint have proven to be invaluable for modern biblical scholars too. They help show how the Bible came together. Further, because they translate ancient copies of the biblical text, they sometimes preserve versions of those texts that may differ from the received Hebrew text. They also give insight into how an ancient Hebrew source text was translated into languages that non-Hebrew readers could understand. In fact, most of the Old Testament quotes that appear in the Greek New Testament come from the Septuagint. In many ways, the Septuagint set the pattern for the other ancient translations of the Bible into Greek, Latin, and Aramaic. Aramaic translations are known as *Targum*, and the earliest examples are partially preserved translations of Leviticus and Job from the Dead Sea Scrolls.

Learned men weren't merely translating the Bible into Greek during this pivotal era. They were also busy writing new, spiritual material.

The account of Susanna is one such story from this period: Two creepy old men secretly watch a young woman take a bath in her back garden and decide to blackmail her. Unless she acquiesces to their lustful desires, they will accuse her of committing adultery. When the honorable Susanna refuses, the men have her arrested and put on trial. Right as this innocent woman is about to be convicted, Daniel—a Jewish teenager who would later become a significant prophetic figure—steps forward. Acting as a kind of detective/defense attorney, young Daniel questions the men separately. When their fabricated stories fail to line up, Susanna is exonerated and the false accusers are put to death.

Do you remember this dramatic story from your childhood religious education? You probably don't if you are a Jew familiar only with the contents of the Hebrew Bible. Indeed, the rabbis of the Talmud seem to have forbidden the reading of these books (even though one book is quoted by them). You may have never seen these books if you are a Protestant who typically reads from a modern Bible translation like the New International Version. This is because the account of Susanna is one of a small number of writings[1] from this era (200–100 BCE) that scholars have puzzled and argued over since the fourth century CE, asking this question: Are these books or accounts truly divinely inspired, or are they merely inspiring works of human origin?

When the Septuagint was originally assembled, the account of Susanna and these other writings were included, no questions asked. But in 382 BCE, Jerome, one of the preeminent scholars of the early Christian church, began wondering about their divine authority.

Jerome had been commissioned to translate the Bible into Latin, the language of the Roman Empire. Jerome felt strongly that only those Old Testament books originally written in Hebrew should be regarded as Scripture. He called Susanna and the rest of these other writings *apocryphal*, which means "obscure" or "things hidden away." (The word has since come to mean "dubious" or "suspect.") At the time, the question was not whether these stories could have happened, but whether the writings met the criteria for canonicity—or being part of the official Bible.

Jerome reluctantly included these books in his Latin Bible translation (called the Vulgate, from a word meaning "common") with a few disclaimers. In subsequent editions of the Vulgate, the disclaimers disappeared. Eventually the books in question were given their own separate section in certain Christian Bibles—between the Old and New Testaments.

Though readers won't find these writings in Jewish or most modern Protestant Bibles, Roman Catholic and Eastern Orthodox Bibles still include them. As mentioned previously, these books are sometimes called *deuterocanonical*, a word that means "second canon" or "added to the canon." In 1546, the Roman Catholic Council of Trent declared these books to be Scripture.

Though theologians and clergy don't agree that these writings are inspired, most admit they are beneficial and make for worthwhile reading. Christopher Columbus certainly found that to be the case. Historians tell us that when Columbus read 2 Esdras 6:42—"On the third day you commanded the waters to be gathered together in a seventh part of the earth; six parts you dried up"—he had this thought: If the earth's surface is six parts dry land and only one part water, then it can't be much of a voyage from the west coast of Europe to the eastern shores of Asia.

Who knew? The Apocrypha, those books viewed as dubious by so many, may actually have played a key role in the discovery of the Americas!

In addition to the creation of the Septuagint and the writing of the Apocrypha, a few other significant biblical events took place during the turbulent Second Temple period.

First, the Hebrew canon was forming. Out of all the scrolls being read and copied and circulated by the Jewish people, consensus was building that certain books were divinely inspired. Typically, these were the books widely viewed as authoritative because they were connected to a recognized prophet or to a priest or king who demonstrated prophetic gifts.

By 450 BCE, the Torah (the first five books of Bible) was universally regarded by Jews as canonical. By 200 BCE, most Jews also deemed the Prophets (the second section of standard Hebrew Bibles) as Scripture. It took a bit longer—until about 200 CE—for the remaining books of the third section of the Tanakh—the Writings—to be widely recognized as sacred Scripture (though there was consensus on most books by 70 CE).

Second, the community at Qumran—the group that left us the Dead Sea Scrolls—formed. Jewish sects such as the Essenes, which many scholars identify with the Qumran community, increasingly disagreed with the political and religious establishment during the Greek and Roman Periods. Many prominent scholars are convinced it was this group that withdrew to the wilderness around the Dead Sea to study and copy their sacred writings. Others see this as a different but closely related group.

Whoever they were, the Qumran community just wanted to be alone. And they were, at least until the marauding Romans showed up in 68 CE with a goal of destroying all Jewish resistance to Roman rule. That's when they stuck their valuable scrolls in pottery jars and stashed them in remote desert caves near the Dead Sea.

These ancient documents remained hidden there for almost 1,900 years, until marauders of a different kind showed up.

CHAPTER FOUR

WHAT THE GOATHERDS FOUND

The Dead Sea Scrolls

Every area on the face of the earth, be it
seemingly ever so waste and empty,
has a story behind it which the inquisitive
sooner or later will attempt to obtain.

—Nelson Glueck, rabbi, archaeologist, and former president of Hebrew Union College

Our best history teachers aren't always PhDs from prestigious schools. Sometimes they are creatures from the wild.

We've already mentioned the partridge that led a bedouin hunter—sometime in the late 1920s or early '30s, best anyone can tell—into a desert cave that had obviously served as a kind of ancient storage room. (More on what was found in that cave in a moment.)

In 2015, it was a porcupine that lent a hand—or, more accurately, a paw. In March, the Israel Antiquities Authority (IAA) reported finding a 1,400-year-old oil lamp at the Emek Hefer excavation in central Israel. How did this valuable artifact suddenly appear?

It seems that porcupines like to make their homes at archaeological sites. In this case, the ceramic lamp was sitting atop a fresh pile of dirt at the entrance to a porcupine burrow. Clearly giddy over this discovery, researchers issued the following tongue-in-cheek statement: "The IAA calls on all porcupines to avoid digging burrows at archeological sites and warns that digging at an archeological site without a license is a criminal offense." (This is one of many moments of levity associated with excavations. And you thought archaeologists were a somber, stuffy bunch!)

Sometime between November 1946 and February 1947, it was a goat that was responsible for perhaps the most important discovery of all.

The essential story is that some Arab teenagers stumbled upon several old scrolls in a cave near the Dead Sea. The young men were from the Tamireh bedouin tribe, well known for their illicit discovery and sale of antiquities. But according to John C. Trever, a Yale-educated archaeologist who conducted interviews with the young men, the whole thing started with a wayward goat.

How bizarre is that? Sometimes it's simply a common critter—not a scholar or a scientist—that helps peel back the pages of the past.

There are dozens of variations on exactly how the Dead Sea Scrolls were discovered, but the best-documented and most popular version goes something like this.

A young Tamireh bedouin goatherd by the name of Muhammed edh-Dibh ("Muhammed the Wolf") was with his cousin Jum'a and another friend in the rocky hills a mile or so from the northwestern shore of the Dead Sea. Late one afternoon, while searching for a stray goat among the limestone cliffs, Jum'a is said to have thrown a stone into a cave opening. But rather than hearing a scared bleat or the clatter of rock striking rock, the young men heard what sounded like pottery shattering! A second throw yielded the same results. They all had the same thought: *If there are pots in the cave, then what might be in the pots?*

Some accounts say Muhammed immediately scrambled up the cliff to investigate. Others say it was too late in the day, and the young men agreed to come back the next morning. Even if we are not sure exactly when "the Wolf" entered the cave, we do know what he found when he did.

The rocky, dusty floor was littered with broken pottery. Amid the debris were several intact jars. They were elongated, about two feet tall. Some still had lids.

With great excitement, "the Wolf" examined the contents of the pots. Nothing in the first nine, and no treasure—at least, not the kind he was hoping for—in the tenth. "All" he found, wrapped in foul-smelling cloth, were some old leather scrolls.

Without stopping to consider that he was likely the first human in more than 1,900 years to lay eyes on these ancient texts, he tucked the parchments under his arms and exited the cave (now referred to as Cave 1, since this was the first of many caves in the area where such written material would be found).

Over the next few months "the Wolf" and his companions approached some antiquities dealers in Bethlehem. In April, one of those men, Khalil Iskander Shahin (nicknamed "Kando"), a Syrian Orthodox Christian, brokered a deal to sell the four scrolls to the Syrian Orthodox Metropolitan (Archbishop) of Jerusalem, a man by the name of Athanasius Samuel. Kando would serve throughout the 1950s as a go-between: purchasing scrolls from the bedouin and selling them to the Jordanian authorities. In November, the bedouin young men allegedly sold another three scrolls they had found to a man named Fiedi Salahi, though the Kando family argues that they entered the market through another (suspect) route. In all, the bedouin are said to have received the modern equivalent of around two or three hundred dollars—for ancient scrolls regarded today as priceless!

Complicating matters for museums and antiquities experts are the claims by some scholars that there have been forgeries on the market—allegedly made from old, blank papyrus found in the caves with the scrolls. The discovery of a "new" Dead Sea Scroll cave in 2017 only added to this intrigue, especially since that cave contained some blank papyrus.

Most people have no clue that the world of ancient manuscripts is, at times, reminiscent of a TV detective drama or a Sherlock Holmes novel. We will look more at this a bit later. Just know that the debate over the status of certain recently acquired Dead Sea Scrolls will rage long after you finish this book.

However, the authenticity of the thousands of Dead Sea Scrolls found in the 1950s is not in question.

When someone informed Eleazar Sukenik, a professor at the Hebrew University in Jerusalem and the founder of the Hebrew University's Institute for Archaeology, about Salahi's purchase from the bedouin teens, he did what any antiquities experts would do—he hastily arranged a meeting to have a look.

But in November 1947, such a meeting was complicated. The city—in fact, the whole region—was on edge. A newly formed entity called the United Nations was preparing to vote on whether to partition Palestine and give the Jewish people their own homeland within what was then British Mandatory Palestine. Though Jews were wild with hope, the very idea outraged Arabs. Tensions were high. Palestine was a powder keg.

Despite this incendiary climate, Sukenik went to his meeting. It was both awkward and quick. He only got to glimpse one of the Dead Sea parchments briefly—and he had to do that through the barbed-wire fence that separated Jerusalem's Arab and Jewish quarters. That quick peek, however, was all he needed. Sukenik recognized the writing on the document as the kind of lettering used back in the first century!

A few days later, on November 29, as the UN delegates convened for their historic vote amid threats of violence and rumors of war, Sukenik knew he had to act. Despite warnings from his son, Yigael Yadin (who was a leader of the Israel Defense Forces), Sukenik embarked on another dangerous bus ride into the Arab sector of Bethlehem. There, while drinking Turkish coffee with Salahi, he struck a deal to purchase the scrolls. Meanwhile, half a world away, in Flushing Meadow, New York, the UN voted to adopt the resolution to partition Palestine and give Israel its own territory. This international effort to foster peace in Palestine resulted in an explosion of rage.

Just to be on the safe side, Archbishop Samuel smuggled his four scrolls to Beirut.

In the incident of the lost goat, the bedouin people saw a cash cow. Never mind that war raged between Arabs and Israelis for all of 1948 and the first half of 1949. Never mind that as the new state of Israel fought for its independence, Jordan invaded the part of Palestine that includes Qumran (known to us as the West Bank)—and would control it until 1967. The

Tamireh tribe continued to scour the desolate cliffs and wadis around the Dead Sea in search of more ancient documents to sell.

At the same time, word of their manuscript discoveries was spreading throughout the academic and religious communities, causing quite a stir. Archaeologists became fixated on the desert east of Jerusalem. They began pulling political strings wherever possible. In 1948, G. L. Harding, the British director of antiquities for Jordan, enlisted the aid of country's Arab Legion to look for caves that might contain scrolls.

From the moment he acquired the four ancient scrolls from Kando in mid-1947, Archbishop Samuel had been trying in vain to figure out exactly what he had purchased. In early 1948, he reached out to John C. Trever, director of the American School of Oriental Research in Jerusalem (now called the W. F. Albright Institute of Archaeological Research).

Trever grabbed his camera and met with the archbishop. He sent photographs of the scrolls to Dr. William F. Albright, the legendary American archaeologist and philologist. Albright was flabbergasted. He figured the scrolls probably originated about 100 BCE—a full thousand years earlier than any other known Old Testament manuscripts! Trembling with excitement, he immediately wired Trever, hailing the documents as the most important manuscript find of the twentieth century.

Meanwhile, in 1949, as the conflict between the Jews and Arabs continued, Archbishop Samuel took his Cave 1 scrolls to the United States. His goal was threefold: to get them out of harm's way, to display them, and to find a buyer.

Simultaneously, a team under the leadership of Roland de Vaux, a Dominican scholar from France and a colleague of G. L. Harding, returned to Cave 1 and began excavating. The bedouin had already retrieved the best treasures, but there were still some goodies to be had. Before they called it quits, de Vaux's team recovered the remains of more than seventy manuscripts. In late 1951, de Vaux decided to move on. He set his sights on a dry plateau below the cave.

De Vaux struck archaeological gold excavating at this site, now known as Khirbet Qumran. Explorers in the mid-1800s had known of a cemetery here—suggesting the existence of some kind of ancient community nearby. Sure enough, de Vaux found the cemetery, containing about 1,200 graves. And that's not all.

He also unearthed the remains of some kind of settlement—an apparent religious commune. Under the dust and rock, he not only found cisterns and hundreds of cups and plates, but he also came across ritual baths and animal bones mixed with pottery—evidence of ritual meals. Another area yielded some inkwells and what may have been a plastered bench, which could suggest a scriptorium (a place where documents were written and copied).

De Vaux found pottery and the remains of kilns used to fire that pottery. And if all that weren't enough, he found more than 1,200 silver and bronze coins. The coins indicated that Qumran was populated up to 68 CE, when it was destroyed.

The local bedouin (who were often hired by archaeologists to help with desert excavation work) were paying close attention. If this ancient community had special rooms for writing and copying documents, and if one stash of documents had already been found in a nearby cave, perhaps other caves in the area had also served as storage units for the settlement.

With their knowledge of the desert, the bedouin intensified their searches—often working at night. Sure enough, in February 1952, they located another cave (Cave 2), containing portions of all five books of the Pentateuch, Psalms, and Jeremiah. Fragments from two noncanonical works, the books of Enoch and Jubilees, were also discovered.

As word leaked out about this find, archaeologists became justifiably concerned. They recoiled at the thought of priceless documents being mishandled, irreparably damaged, held for ransom, or possibly lost forever. In response, they stepped up their efforts to search every cave in the area. The rewards came quickly. The following month, Cave 3 was discovered.

In addition to yielding fragments from a dozen or so scrolls—a mix of biblical and extrabiblical works—the real treasure from Cave 3 was the document known as the Copper Scroll. Dated to the early first century CE, this unique metallic document lists sixty-four secret sites where items of gold and silver—from the temple, some have speculated—and copper are supposedly hidden. (It is worth noting that none of these supposed treasures has ever been found, despite the fervent efforts of numerous treasure hunters.)

In August 1952, a group of young bedouin goatherds was sitting around a fire talking excitedly about the caves of Qumran—all the things being discovered, all the treasures that must be out there for the taking. After listening for a while, an older man in the group began relating a story from his youth.

Decades before, while hunting in the area, he had winged a desert partridge. The wounded bird had flapped and fluttered into a cliffside cave. When he pursued the bird, he had discovered pottery and other artifacts. The younger men leaned forward in excitement. "Do you remember where the cave was?" they asked. "Could you take us there?"

The old man nodded.

That's how Cave 4 was found—barely two hundred yards from the dig then underway at Qumran. Perhaps the most famous of the Dead Sea caves, Cave 4 contained a treasure trove of ancient writings—more than 15,000 manuscript fragments from more than 200 works.

Working covertly at night, the bedouin took from the cave both biblical and extrabiblical texts, plus commentaries on Jewish law. They found tefillin (the leather boxes that Jewish men wear on their foreheads and arms) and mezuzot (parchments inscribed with verses from the Torah and mounted on the doorpost). The bedouin sold the majority of these fragments to Kando. He, in turn, sold them to the Palestine Archeological Museum (now known as the Rockefeller Museum). By the time archaeologists caught wind of this document-filled cave right under their noses, only about 20% of the original material was left.

Though Cave 4 yielded a great quantity of fragments, they were not well preserved. Many were tiny, some containing no more than a few letters. They were brittle, often worm eaten, and corroded by bat droppings. Many were blackened with age. Frank M. Cross, a Harvard scholar later tasked with trying to identify and preserve these antiquities, said most were so fragile they could "scarcely be touched with a camel's-hair brush."[1] Experts are now using computer technology to try to place some of these smaller remaining biblical jigsaw puzzle pieces, more than sixty years after their discovery.

Through 1956, teams of archaeologists and groups of bedouin tribesmen continued to compete in seeking out caves near the Qumran settlement that might contain ancient texts. In all, eleven

Qumran caves have been found to contain document fragments—some 80,000 in all. These come from more than 900 distinct scrolls, about 230 of which are biblical.

These ancient writings are of all sizes and conditions. The Temple Scroll, found in Cave 11, is the longest of the scrolls, measuring 26.7 feet (8.148 meters).

Through carbon-14 dating techniques and also by examining lettering styles, scholars have concluded that most of these manuscripts or manuscript pieces were originally copied between around 225 BCE and 50 CE.

Almost all historians are now in agreement that the caves (and their contents) and the excavated community below are connected. In fact, the consensus is that the scrolls comprised the library of those who inhabited the Qumran settlement.

This success at Qumran sparked a broader search that continued into the 1960s. In caves to the south (in the Judean desert), whole caches of documents were discovered at Masada, the last holdout of the Jewish revolt, one of the most traumatic endings of any battle in history (73 CE). Manuscript fragments were discovered in a storage area outside the synagogue there and in one of the chambers of the casemate wall.

As mentioned above, in early 2017, excited researchers announced the discovery of a twelfth Dead Sea Scrolls cave. Although no scrolls were found inside the cave, Dr. Oren Gutfeld of the Hebrew University of Jerusalem revealed that the cave contained broken storage jars and lids, plus blank writing material, scroll wrappings, and a string that tied the scrolls. Archaeologists also found a couple of iron pickaxe heads (ca. 1950), suggesting the cave had been looted.

When scholars piece together these world-famous scrolls and translate them, what do they find?

About 25% of the documents are copies of biblical books. In fact, the scrolls found at Qumran include all or part of every book of the Tanakh (the Hebrew Bible, or Old Testament) except for the book of Esther.

The majority of these texts are written in Hebrew or Aramaic, although a few are in Greek. Among the other documents found are various commentaries on the Scriptures. There are some hymns and prayers, plus prophetic writings that feature apocalyptic imagery and references to a great war at the end of time between the Sons of Light (Righteousness) and the Sons of Darkness. Other documents are more mundane. They contain very specific rules and instructions for how the Qumran community was expected to function on a day-to-day basis. No New Testament texts were found. This reflects two realities: the timing of Qumran's demise (68 CE, when Christians were still in the process of writing their founding documents) and the fact that there is no evidence that Christians were part of the Qumran community.

Over the years, some have wondered if the settlement at Qumran could have been a fortress or military outpost, or perhaps a villa owned by a wealthy person. A careful analysis of all the facts and clues found at Qumran screams, "This is where a Jewish sect once lived." Archaeological evidence reveals a group of people choosing to shun the world, live in a remote desert location, study Hebrew texts, and pursue lives of piety and moral purity.

A case can be made that the inhabitants may have been a splinter group of Sadducees who regarded themselves as the true sons of Zadok (the chief priest during the days of David and Solomon). If so, they would have been appalled at the illegitimate Hasmonean takeover of the priesthood in 152 BCE. Those political developments, plus their sharp theological differences with the Pharisees and their cultural concerns over the Hellenization of the nation, would have been enough for the group to withdraw. Given the found scrolls' heavy emphasis on the Torah and stress on keeping temple traditions, this theory has merit.

However, the majority of scholars agree that Qumran was likely populated by Essenes. Though this group is not mentioned in the New Testament or in rabbinic literature, historians talk at length about the Essenes. Pliny the Elder, a noted Roman philosopher and author, described the Essenes as an ascetic group that eschewed material possessions, practiced celibacy, and lived by the Dead Sea. The Jewish historian Josephus described the sect as living in a communal arrangement, pursuing piety, studying the sacred writings, and observing the Sabbath together.

Whatever the origin of the Qumran community, this much is beyond debate: when they grew weary of what they perceived as a corrupt, compromised Judaism in Jerusalem, they packed up their belongings and their beloved holy scrolls, and they moved to this solitary area adjacent to the Dead Sea. There they lived from roughly 100 BCE until 68 CE.

It is strange to consider that on the same day Jesus stood in the temple in Jerusalem debating the law with the Sadducees and Pharisees, members of this devout group were *reading* the law in the desert just twenty-four miles to the southeast. As Paul was visiting synagogues across Asia Minor to try to convince Jews that Jesus was the promised Messiah, the community of Qumran was at that moment speculating about and waiting for the Messiah's arrival. There is, however, no proof of a historical connection between the Jesus of the New Testament and the "Teacher of Righteousness" or "Messiah" mentioned in the Qumran community's documents.

Interest in the Dead Sea Scrolls continued well beyond the shores of the Dead Sea.

On June 1, 1954, the Syrian Orthodox Metropolitan (Archbishop) Samuel placed an ad in the *Wall Street Journal* that read: "The Four Dead Sea Scrolls: Biblical manuscripts dating back to at least 200 BC are for sale. This would be an ideal gift to an educational or religious institution by an individual or group. Box F206."

Yigael Yadin saw the ad. Remember him—the high-ranking leader in the Israel Defense Force? By 1954 he was following in the footsteps of his famous archaeologist father, Eleazar Sukenik. (Sukenik had died the previous year without realizing his dream of reuniting all seven scrolls from Cave 1.)

Yadin didn't hesitate. Without revealing his involvement publicly, he arranged to buy the scrolls on behalf of Israel. He paid $250,000 for all four—considered one of the great bargains in history. Thus in 1955, he united the four scrolls he had purchased with the three acquired by his father six years earlier. At last, all seven scrolls were together again in their native Israel.

In 1965, the scrolls were moved from the Hebrew University of Jerusalem to the newly constructed Shrine of the Book of the Israel Museum in Jerusalem. This museum, two-thirds of which is underground, is built in the shape of the top of one of the Dead Sea scroll jars.

Meticulous. Careful. Deliberate. Painstaking. Perfectionist.

As a general rule, scholars in the field of archaeology are all these things. Before they go public with a new find, they want to study it carefully and understand exactly what it is they have discovered.

The Dead Sea Scrolls team was no different. Led by Father Roland de Vaux, it was an international "all-star team" of young scholars. Jozef Milik from Poland was fluent in nineteen languages. The eccentric Englishman John Allegro later gained notoriety (and lost credibility) for his book claiming that Christianity had begun as a shamanistic, hallucinogenic cult. John Strugnell, another Brit, ultimately devoted four decades of his life to the study of the scrolls.

Poring long and hard over each fragment meant that information about the scrolls was leaking out at a snail's pace—a small exhibit here, a few photos there. Occasional lectures and articles weren't enough to satisfy demand. A stream of press releases had reported the finding of these ancient documents. Why wasn't de Vaux's team publishing its discoveries? Why was it taking so long?

Conspiracy theorists came out of the woodwork. Scholars, they claimed—under pressure from the church—were engaged in a massive cover-up.

In bits and pieces, the manuscript finds were published, but the pace was way too slow. When East Jerusalem passed into Israeli control as a result of the Six-Day War in 1967, the team for publishing the scrolls remained in place but still published very little. International pressure began to build and eventually led in 1990 to a series of steps leading to the release of bootleg texts of the unpublished scrolls. First, two scholars from the Hebrew Union College in Cincinnati released reconstructions of the texts based on a concordance, an index of words, prepared by the publication team. Shortly afterward, the Huntington Library in California released microfilm copies of photographic negatives stored in their vaults for safekeeping. Finally, bootleg copies of the photos kept in the Palestine Archaeological Museum appeared—although to this day we do not know how these photographs were obtained. All three of these bootleg editions were published by the Biblical Archaeological Society, whose editor, Hershel Shanks, played a leading role in the campaign to release the full corpus of manuscripts.

Finally, in 1990 the Israel Antiquities Authority stepped in. It officially opened access to the entire corpus of photographic images and reorganized the publication process under the leadership of Emanuel Tov of the Hebrew University. This led, at last, to the full publication of the Dead Sea Scrolls. Tov and his colleagues also implemented various electronic and digital tools for studying the Dead Sea Scrolls and related texts.

Finding the Dead Sea Scrolls was a landmark event for both historians and biblical scholars.

Historically, the scrolls give us a peek into a pivotal era of Judaism. Forged during the latter part of the Second Temple period (ca. 225 BCE to 70 CE), the extrabiblical scrolls (such as the Community Rule Scroll, found in Cave 1) reveal the beliefs and practices of a separatist group that was apparently infuriated with the prevailing religious establishment in Jerusalem. Those leaders were seen as corrupt—too liberal in their beliefs, too cozy with Hellenistic ideas, too lax in their adherence to ancient temple rituals. The Habakkuk Commentary from Cave 1 and manuscripts of the Damascus Document from Cave 4 include scathing denunciations of the corrupt leaders of the Jewish temple. The War Scroll

These four scholars greatly influenced efforts to bring the Bible to the masses. Clockwise from top left: Luther, Erasmus, Maimonides, Wycliffe.

Constantin von Tischendorf (1815–1874), German
biblical scholar who discovered the Codex Sinaiticus.

Saint Catherine's Monastery, located at the foot of Mount Sinai, Egypt. An Eastern Orthodox monastery (established in 565 CE). The Codex Sinaiticus was discovered here in 1844 by Constantin von Tischendorf.

ΘΡΗΝΟΙ
ΙΕΡΕΜΙΟΥ

Codex Sinaiticus (ca. 330–360 CE), a handwritten copy on parchment of the Greek Bible. Considered one of the best Greek texts of the New Testament..

Top: Cave in Qumran, where some of the Dead Sea Scrolls were initially discovered. ***Right bottom:*** Two Dead Sea Scrolls discovered in the twentieth century. ***Left bottom:*** Clay jar that held some of the scroll fragments.

בקומו לערוץ הארץ חדלו לכמה מן האדם אשר נשמה
באפו כיא במה נחשב הואה
כיא הנה האדון יהוה צבאות מסיר מירושלים ומיהודה
משען ומשענה כול משען לחם וכול משען מים גבור ואיש
מלחמה שופט ונביא וקוסם וזקן שר חמשים ונשוא פנים
ויועץ וחכם חרשים ונבון לחש ונתתי נערים שריהמה
ותעלולים ימשולו בם ונגש העם איש באיש ואיש ברעהו
ירהבו הנער בזקן והנקלה בנכבד כיא יתפוש איש באחיהו
בית אביו שמלה לכה קצין תהיה לנו והמכשלה הזואת
תחת ידכה וישא ביום ההוא לאמור לוא אהיה חובש
ובביתי אין לחם ואין שמלה לוא תשימוני קצין עם כי כשלה
ירושלים ויהודה נפלה כיא לשונם ומעלליהם על יהוה להמרות
עיני כבודו הכרת פניהם ענתה בם וחטאתם כסדום הגידו
ולוא כחדו אוי לנפשם כיא גמלו להם רעה אמרו צדיק
כיא טוב כיא פרי מעלליהם יואכלו אוי לרשע רע כיא
גמול ידיו יעשה לו עמי נוגשו מעולל ונשים משלו בו עמי
מאשריך מתעים ודרך ארחותיך בלעו
נצב לריב יהוה ועומד לדין עמים יהוה במשפט יבוא עם
זקני עמו ושריו ואתמה בערתם הכרם גזלת העני בבתיכמה
אדוני
מה לכמה תדכאו עמי ופני עניים תטחנו נואם אדוני יהוה
צבאות
ויואמר יהוה יען כיא גבהו בנות ציון ותלכנה נטוות
גרון ומשקרות עיניהם הלוך וטפוף תלכנה וברגליהמה
ויהוה
תעכסנה ושפח אדוני קדקוד בנות ציון ויהוה פותהן
אדוני
יערה ביום ההוא יסיר יהוה את תפארת העכסים
והשביסים והשהרונים והנטפות והשרות והרעלות
והפארים והצעדות והקשורים ובתי הנפש והלחשים
והטבעות ונזמי האף המחלצות והמעטפות והמטפחות
והגליונים והסדינים והצנופות והרדידים והיה

The Great Isaiah Scroll (1Qlsa), Dead Sea Scroll. Found in Cave 1 (Qumran) by bedouin shepherds in 1947. It is the oldest and most complete copy of the book of Isaiah in existence.

Eleazar Sukenik (1889–1953), Israeli archaeologist, professor at the Hebrew University of Jerusalem, and author. He worked tirelessly to purchase the Dead Sea Scrolls for the State of Israel.

from Cave 1 prophesizes a victory of the Sons of Light (or Righteousness) over the Sons of Darkness—Gentile oppressors and Jews who do not join the scrolls sect.

For the last sixty years, supermarket tabloids have teased shoppers with headlines such as "The Explosive Secrets of the Dead Sea Scrolls." To hear these rags (and even some book authors) tell it, the ancient Jewish scrolls found near Qumran contain all sorts of bombshells: the truth about UFOs, maps to the Lost City of Atlantis or the Fountain of Youth. Like clockwork, such ridiculous claims appear . . . supposed prophecies about Hitler, alleged clues about when the world will end, miracle Bible diets that *really* work, ad nauseam.

The scrolls contain no such things. So, what do the Dead Sea Scrolls reveal?

The Qumran collection includes parts of all the books of the Hebrew Bible except the book of Esther, which may not have been accepted as authoritative by the sect. Or, it is possible that its brevity—only ten chapters—may have led to its absence among the remains, especially when we consider the fragmentary condition of many of the scrolls.

We learn from the scrolls a tremendous amount about scribal practices and methods by which the Hebrew Scriptures were passed down in ancient times. We also learn that alongside the Masoretic Text (the text deemed as the authoritative, official Hebrew Bible text in the Common Era), manuscripts circulated that reflected other text forms, such as that which underlies the Greek translation in the Septuagint. Further, scribes sometimes included expansions and interpretations in their copies. Nonetheless, the Dead Sea Scrolls assure us, despite the minor textual variations, that the biblical texts that we use today are virtually the same in wording and content as the ancient texts read and studied at Qumran.

What do the Dead Sea Scrolls tell us about Judaism? The scrolls reveal the tremendous intellectual and religious ferment that existed in the second and first centuries BCE. Debates swirled about issues related to Jewish law, ritual, theology, and messianism. Prominent among these issues were the debates between the Pharisees on one side, and the Sadducean party and Qumran sect on the other side, pertaining to many issues of Jewish law. Also prominent was the assumption that the end of days was about to dawn. Many of these issues help us to understand the development of Judaism from the Second Temple period into the Judaism of the Talmudic rabbis that remains the basis for the Judaism of today.

The Dead Sea Scrolls don't say anything about Christianity or Jesus, though they do display a sect with strong Messianic expectation. There is zero evidence in the scrolls that the residents of Qumran were a Christian sect, or that John the Baptist was a member of this group, or that Jesus was the "Teacher of Righteousness" referred to in some of the fragments.

As far as Christianity is concerned, the Dead Sea Scrolls provide a historical window into the social-political-religious climate of Palestine leading up to the ministry of Jesus and the birth of the church. This helps us understand specific ideas and passages found in the New Testament. Further, they give us a good idea of the Bible Jesus would have used—and the one we all use as well.

Qumran is not only important for historians, but it is of major significance for biblical scholarship. The scrolls shed light on how the Old Testament was formed and transmitted through the ages. In the Dead Sea Scroll material, we find a disproportionate number of scrolls of books of the Torah, especially Genesis and Deuteronomy. There are twenty-one copies of Isaiah and thirty-six of the Psalms. By noting the books the community most often quoted, copied, and preserved, scholars get a picture of the books held in highest esteem.

Also, the biblical texts found at Qumran are not identical—there are discrepancies. To look at it another way: it is like the modern use of different translations. Observe the various types of Bibles in a typical gathering of the faithful, from the New International Version and English Standard Version, to the New American Bible and New Jerusalem Bible, to the Stone Tanakh and the Jewish Publication Society translations. Who can explain why one is used or preferred over another? Likewise, we will never fully know the reasons for the variations among Qumran texts.

These manuscripts, together with scroll fragments from Masada and other nearby sites, help us trace the initial efforts of Jewish scribes to standardize the Hebrew Bible. It was this work that led to the creation of the Masoretic Hebrew text, which became the authoritative text of the Hebrew Bible.

When you were a kid, you likely played the "Telephone" game. You whispered something into the ear of the person next to you—something like, "I have a big, black dog that likes to eat potatoes." As the secret was repeated three or four times, it morphed. At the end of the game, the person at the end of the line revealed what he or she had heard—"I went out back and found a frog in my tomatoes"—and everybody enjoyed a good laugh.

This is the inherent danger when information is passed on orally or even in written form. Without a copy machine, stories must be shared verbally or recopied by hand. The more this is done, the more opportunities there are for mistakes to occur. A word gets changed here; a fact gets added there. This letter gets confused. That line gets left out. Before long, the latest version is nothing like the original.

If you are playing a silly parlor game, this is no big deal. If you are seeking to transmit vital information accurately, a garbled message is a huge deal.

For centuries, it was this human propensity to make mistakes that caused heartburn for students of the Bible. Skeptics were quick to ask, How do you know that the people who copied the Scriptures were careful? How can you be sure they didn't change things they didn't like? What if the biblical documents we read today are nothing like the originals?

Before the Dead Sea Scroll discoveries, nobody had clear answers to such questions. The only known early Hebrew texts were the four fragments of the Nash papyrus (ca. 100 BCE), which were just a glimpse of biblical passages—but at least included the Ten Commandments. In 1945, the oldest known manuscript of the Hebrew Bible other than these pieces was the Aleppo Codex (930 CE). Clearly, a document that is 1,000 years old is ancient! Yet the Aleppo Codex was still more than 1,300 years removed from the end of the Hebrew Bible storyline (ca. 400 BCE). Unfortunately, the claim that the Cairo Codex, long kept in the Karaite synagogue in Cairo and now located in Jerusalem, could be dated according to its colophon to 895 CE has been disproven by carbon dating, so the Aleppo Codex remains the earliest known manuscript beside the Nash papyrus previous to the discovery of the Dead Sea Scrolls.

Think of that—a thirteen-century gap between the original writing and the earliest copy of that writing. That's thirteen centuries of copying and recopying, thirteen centuries for all sorts of errors to creep in. If five kids can butcher a simple sentence in sixty seconds while sitting together in the same room, then could it be that the Hebrew Scriptures were mangled and distorted over more than a millennium of copying?

It took a stray goat to alleviate such worries. First, his owner, a bedouin goatherd nicknamed "the Wolf," emerged from a desert cave with an armload of scrolls. Second, scholars were able to determine that one of those scrolls—a scroll of Isaiah—had been copied in 125 BCE. (That's around 1,000 years older than the Aleppo Codex.) Third, scholars were able to compare the two manuscripts to see exactly how many differences there were between the Dead Sea Scrolls and the Aleppo Codex—separated by ten-plus centuries.

Do you know what they found? In most instances of textual comparison, the two scrolls were found to be almost identical. The discrepancies that did exist were mostly the result of different spellings and dialectic conventions. A few others were scribal errors and some constituted small variants in the text. To be fair, a few manuscripts, while passing on the same moral and religious message, showed significant changes: A seemingly different edition of a book. A different order of the book's passages. But overall, the Dead Sea Scroll discoveries helped validate the reliability of the transmission process of the Hebrew Scriptures through the ages. At the same time, they show that prior to the standardization of the text in the first century CE, some biblical texts did indeed exhibit some significant variance with those in the texts later declared authoritative, termed the Masoretic ("traditional") Text.

This much is clear: The copying of sacred texts and the process of determining which reading was authoritative were not a parlor game for the Jewish people. This was a very serious business practiced with the utmost care and precision.

This is why Constantin von Tischendorf was poking around the area considered by many to be Sinai looking for ancient manuscripts in the 1840s and '50s. It's also what motivated archaeologists a century later to comb desert caves around the Dead Sea—and haggle with goatherds to get their hands on old biblical documents.

Each time we find a text of the Bible that is older than any we have ever seen, we get nearer to the original writings of Scripture.

As we have previously pointed out, the ancient tradition of Judaism is to take old biblical manuscripts and bury them in a reverent way so that the pieces of literature considered holy are able to return to the dust of the earth. This, plus the passage of time, gives insight into why we have none of the original biblical manuscripts.

It's obvious that the scrolls and fragments found at Qumran weren't buried; they were hidden. They weren't being retired; they were being protected. Around 68 CE, some were hurriedly placed into clay pots, and others were put on shelves in hard-to-access caves as the Roman army was steamrolling its way toward the community.

This was the more cumbersome, first-century version of trying to store one's important data in the digital cloud. The inhabitants of Qumran were trying to preserve and protect vital information. They knew what we know: losing important data (whether digital or physical) is devastating.

Mysteriously, no one from Qumran ever returned to fetch these precious scrolls. Thankfully, others did before it was too late.

CHAPTER FIVE

"GOSPEL TRUTH"

JESUS AND THE EVANGELISTS

But there are also many other things that Jesus did; if every one of them were written down, I suppose that the world itself could not contain the books that would be written.

—THE APOSTLE JOHN (JOHN 21:25)

It sounds like a fairy tale: "Once upon a time, two poor farmers were digging in the ground, when all of a sudden . . ."

Except that this story is true. It happened on a December day in 1945. It happened at an actual place—about three miles north of Nag Hammadi, Egypt. The men involved were real—Muhammed Al-Samman and his brother Khalifah.

These brothers had traveled by camel to this site along the Nile River because it was known, at least among the locals, for its *sabakh*, a nutrient-rich soil used to fertilize crops. It would become famous for something more than dirt.

At some point in their labors, one of the men's mattocks struck something solid. Some more eager but careful digging unearthed a red, sealed jar. Initially, the men were afraid to open the container, for fear of releasing a *jin* (an evil spirit). But soon curiosity—and the prospect of having discovered a buried treasure—got the better of them. They decided to examine the contents of the jar.

By smashing it open, they unleashed a storm of academic controversy and biblical intrigue.

Inside the jar were thirteen leather-bound papyrus codices (ancient bound books that often contain multiple manuscripts in one volume) written in Coptic, a late dialect of ancient Egyptian that is written in a script adapted from Greek. The official story is that when the men got home and showed their mother what they had found, she became afraid. When they left, she burned some of the 1,600-year-old manuscripts, thinking they might bring bad luck! The brothers later rescued the rest, in hopes of being able to sell them.

About this same time, the brothers brutally murdered the man who had killed their father. Fearful that the police might question them and search their home, they entrusted the ancient codices to the care of a Coptic priest. The priest's brother-in-law, figuring that any books that old must be extremely valuable, took one of the codices to Cairo to show a doctor friend. The doctor notified authorities at the Egyptian Department of Antiquities, who seized the book (paying the brother-in-law a small price) and placed it in the Coptic Museum in Cairo.

In the world of ancient documents, an unexpected discovery and sale like this gets the attention of scholars, antique dealers, church leaders, and government officials. A wide assortment of characters (with varying amounts of character) was attracted by the news of newly discovered texts. Suddenly, illiterate neighbors and money-grubbing merchants, all hoping to make a fast buck, were trying to locate and acquire the documents.

Yet, somehow, despite all the intrigue—and despite all these different players, each with his own agenda—the fifty-two surviving manuscripts (later dated to about 350 CE) ended up in the possession of the Coptic Museum by 1952. They became known as the Nag Hammadi library.

Scholar James Robinson has speculated that these texts may have come from a monastery near Nag Hammadi—that perhaps they were buried in the mid-fourth century after Athanasius, the controversial bishop of Alexandria, sent out his annual letter in which he set forth a list of writings regarded as biblical (canonical) and condemned the use of all other books.

So, what's in these ancient books that someone would bury them? There are various accounts of Jesus and some previously "hidden" gospels and unknown writings. The Nag Hammadi manuscripts include a Gospel of Thomas and a Gospel of Mary and a Gospel of Truth. These cryptic texts contain alleged words and works of Jesus that are not found in the Gospels of the Christian Bible—Matthew, Mark, Luke, and John.

Why weren't these works regarded as biblical? We will discuss that in more detail in the next chapter, but simply put, the Nag Hammadi texts are infused with the spiritual, mystical philosophy of Gnosticism. From the Greek word *gnosis*, which means "knowledge," Gnosticism teaches, among other things, that salvation comes through a secret knowledge that is granted only to an elite few. The Christian apologist Irenaeus (130–202 CE) condemned, for instance, the Apocryphon of John. It describes the Old Testament Creator God negatively in comparison to the unknowable Father of Jesus in the New Testament. This text and others like it, such as the Gospel of Judas, survive today only in Coptic manuscripts. Those texts in the corpus that were biblical in nature weren't necessarily competing with the canon but were built upon it and give views that many deemed problematic.

The Gospel of Thomas is, arguably, the most famous of the Nag Hammadi manuscripts. It is not as tinged with Gnostic beliefs as, perhaps, some of the other works, but it does begin this way: "These are the hidden words that the living Jesus spoke. And Didymos Judas Thomas wrote them down. And he said, 'Whoever finds the meaning of these words will not taste death.'"

Though a few of these Nag Hammadi manuscripts were published in the years following their discovery, it wasn't until 1977 that all the manuscripts were published in English. Two years later, Elaine Pagels, a religious history professor at Princeton, released her critically acclaimed, yet controversial, book on the texts called *The Gnostic Gospels*. This and similar works argue that Gnosticism existed before Christianity and that the Gnostic Gospels preserve authentic traditions stemming from the first generations of the Jesus movement. Other scholars, such as Edwin Yamauchi at Miami University, disagree with the claim of a pre-Christian Gnosticism and see the Gnostic Christian writings as reflecting the views of later groups whose theology was rejected by mainstream Christianity. Suffice it to say, the study of these textual matters involves considerable effort.

In *The Gnostic Gospels*, Elaine Pagels poses some pointed questions about the criteria used for recognizing certain writings as canonical and deeming others unworthy of inclusion in the Christian New Testament: "Who made that selection, and for what reasons? Why were these other writings [the Nag Hammadi library] excluded and banned as 'heresy'?"[1]

These are fair questions, worth examining. But perhaps there are more basic questions: Why are there any Gospels at all? Or put another way: Why did some Jewish followers of Jesus in the first century feel the need to add to the Tanakh—to claim biblical status for a whole new batch of writings that Christians now refer to as the New Testament?

After more than 500 years of almost continuous foreign domination—Persia, followed by Greece, followed by Rome—the Jews of Palestine were restless. Hopes for the arrival of the Messiah (the powerful deliverer-king understood by Second Temple Jews to be alluded to by the Jewish prophets) were at a fever pitch during the first decades of the Common Era.

Around 27 CE, a Galilean called Jesus of Nazareth began turning heads. Though his résumé wasn't much—he was only a carpenter by training—he had a growing reputation as a miracle worker. He also had a way with words. A gifted storyteller, he talked in colorful and cryptic ways about the kingdom of God, which he declared was coming soon.

Yet Jesus was unpredictable and enigmatic. He seemed less bothered by the Roman occupation and more bugged by the religious situation in Jerusalem. Because of his frequent clashes with the scribes, Pharisees, and Sadducees, many Jews assumed things would end badly for Jesus. Israel's First Temple-period prophets had also met with resistance. What's more, the Romans had already executed several aspiring prophetic and messianic figures since taking control of Judea in 63 BCE.

Jesus's most devoted followers, however, saw him as much more than a prophet. They filled their New Testament writings with claims that Jesus was, in fact, Israel's long-awaited Messiah (in Greek, *Christos*, translated "Christ"). In some instances, the New Testament shows this title bestowed on Jesus by his followers (Matthew 1:1; Luke 9:20; John 1:41; Acts 2:36). In other places, Jesus is described as making the claim himself (Matthew 26:63–64; Luke 24:46–48; John 4:25–26).

Another title used by and about Jesus was the label "Son of God" (Mark 1:1; Luke 22:70; John 19:7). With this title, the apostles meant that Jesus was God incarnate (John 1:1–14). To most

Jews, the thought was blasphemous (Matthew 26:65; John 10:33). To most Greeks, it was ludicrous (Acts 17:32).

After three years, many felt Jesus was getting too bold in his proclamations and too pointed in his criticisms. Those in power decided they had heard enough. Pilate, the Roman governor, ordered Jesus's execution.

Just like that, in about 30 CE, the Jesus movement was crushed.

Only it wasn't.

The Acts of the Apostles is a written record of the growth of the Christian church until about the year 60. It was composed late in the first century from oral and written sources circulating in the church—similar to the way oral and written sources had circulated among the Jewish people prior to the writing of the Hebrew Bible (Old Testament).

According to the book of Acts, the Jesus movement didn't die when he died; it sprang to life when he rose from the dead. Only days after Jesus's crucifixion and burial, his followers were steadfastly alleging that Jesus had come back from the dead!

The Christian movement was built on a firm belief in the historicity of Jesus's life, death, and resurrection. The well-known work *The Decline and Fall of the Roman Empire*, though overall antagonistic to Christianity, highlights Christians' belief in these events as central to the movement's growth and resilience, and in turn, crucial to the unfolding of world history.[2]

About seven weeks after Jesus's reported resurrection—and during the celebration of the Jewish festival of *Shavuot* (the Feast of Pentecost) in Jerusalem—the book of Acts says that participants witnessed and experienced supernatural phenomena.

The apostle Peter, speaking on behalf of the small sect of Jesus devotees, explained these miraculous signs as the fulfillment of a prophecy made centuries earlier by the Jewish prophet Joel. Peter claimed these things were proof that Jesus was "both Lord and Messiah" (Acts 2:36).

Even though this message infuriated Jewish authorities, it began to spread like wildfire. Even when threatened with punishment or death, the followers of Jesus (known as "disciples" or "Christians") continued to declare this *gospel* ("good news") with missionary zeal. They became *evangelists* ("those who announce good news"). The content of their message was that Jesus was and remains the Savior sent from God. They maintained that he would return soon in triumph to establish the kingdom of God on earth. They proclaimed this message boldly, not only in Jerusalem and Judea at a time when most Jews in Judea and the Galilee rejected his Messiahship, but—when persecution intensified—to other cultures and a growing non-Jewish audience.

The primary propagators of the Christian movement were Jesus's twelve, handpicked *apostles* ("sent ones"). For about three years, they had been devoted followers of Jesus—his apprentices or protégés, if you will. Now—minus Judas, who had betrayed Jesus and, according to the account in Matthew, committed suicide—they were leading a new, mostly Jewish-Christian sect that would eventually become known as the *church*. Early Christian sources say these "sent ones" fanned out across the globe—Syria, Persia, Asia, Africa, Europe, even to India—to fulfill the command Jesus had given them to "go . . . and make disciples of all nations" (Matthew 28:19).

According to the book of Acts, the leading spokesman for this Christian movement (at least in the early days) was the apostle Peter. He mostly focused his message on the Jewish audience in and around Jerusalem. In time, however, an unlikely thirteenth apostle arrived on the scene: Saul of Tarsus.

The New Testament narrative paints a vivid picture of Saul as an angry man—a devout Pharisee and violent enemy of the Christian message. It then describes his remarkable transformation via an unexpected, supernatural encounter with the resurrected Jesus on the road to Damascus:

> As he was going along and approaching Damascus, suddenly a light from heaven flashed around him. He fell to the ground and heard a voice saying to him, "Saul, Saul, why do you persecute me?" He asked, "Who are you, Lord?" The reply came, "I am Jesus, whom you are persecuting. But get up and enter the city, and you will be told what you are to do." The men who were traveling with him stood speechless because they heard the voice but saw no

> one. Saul got up from the ground, and though his eyes were open, he could see nothing; so they led him by the hand and brought him into Damascus. (Acts 9:3–8)

In a flash, Saul went from being the church's fiercest opponent to being its most faithful proponent. Everything about him—including his name—changed. For the rest of his days, steeped in the Hebrew Scriptures and bearing the message of salvation by grace through faith in Jesus, Paul traveled throughout the Roman Empire, preaching Jesus as the Christ, establishing churches, and writing letters to those churches and church leaders.

What had begun as a sect within Judaism was becoming a separate religion.

Now you know why we have the ancient faith of Judaism and, springing from it, a newer faith known as Christianity. Now you know why we have a Jewish Bible and also a Christian Bible (which features all the books of the Jewish Bible but then adds a few others).

In brief, some Jews in the first century of the Common Era became utterly convinced that Jesus of Nazareth was the Messiah who, in their view, was alluded to in the Jewish Law and Writings and promised in the Hebrew Prophets. Most other Jews did not then (and do not now) share this belief or the particular interpretations of Scripture upon which it is based. They saw the claim that Jesus was divine as being at odds with the Jewish teaching of monotheism. They could not accept the gospel message.

Since about the time those Gnostic texts were written and copied and buried in the rich earth at Nag Hammadi—at least as far anyone can tell—Christian Bibles have included four, and only four, accounts of the life and message of Jesus. Matthew, Mark, Luke, and John all tell essentially the same story, but each provides a unique perspective.

Matthew, Mark, and Luke are called the *Synoptic* Gospels. (*Synoptic* comes from a Greek word that means "to see with" or "to see together.") In other words, these three Gospels take a similar, but not identical view of Jesus. They repeat many of the same teachings and stories. Readers often ask, "Why do we need all three? How, if at all, are they different?"

At the risk of oversimplifying, Matthew takes a more Jewish approach than the others. In his New Testament Gospel, he frequently quotes from the Tanakh. He does this to make a case for Jesus being the long-awaited Messiah and king of the Jews. Because Jews hungered so deeply for the kingdom of God, Matthew included many of Jesus's teachings about the coming kingdom.

Mark is the shortest, most action-packed Gospel. Perhaps written largely for a Roman audience, it depicts Jesus as the ultimate servant to humankind.

The Gospel of Luke seems to be aimed at Greek (or Gentile) believers—and it shows Jesus as the ideal man and the savior of all people.

John is not one of the Synoptic Gospels. It is more theological and evangelistic than the other three Gospels. Near the end of the book, the apostle spells out his motive for writing—that readers "may come to believe that Jesus is the Messiah, the Son of God, and that through believing you may have life in his name" (John 20:31).

When were these four Gospels originally composed? There is no consensus answer to that question. About the only thing scholars agree on is that John is surely the latest, written around the end of the first century. Many are convinced that Mark is the earliest of the Synoptics, dating from the late 60s CE, and that Matthew and Luke were written sometime around 80 CE (or later), using Mark as one of their sources. Traditional Christian scholars dispute these later dates. They contend that the Synoptic Gospels were all written before 70 CE, perhaps as early as 50–60 CE.

Either way, there is a twenty- to fifty-year gap between the events described in the Gospels (say, for example, the crucifixion of Christ) and the written accounts of those events. This prompts the question: How were the facts of Jesus's life accurately preserved during this gap?

When something good happens to you—you get a raise, or you get the chance to go on a fabulous vacation—no one has to remind or nag you to go around telling others. You rush to your smartphone or social media, and you announce your good fortune. It's human nature to talk about life-changing events (sometimes, sadly, to the point of obnoxiousness).

A common explanation given by Christians about the events of Jesus highlights this aspect of human nature. Christians say that, based on their life-changing experiences, his followers began to talk excitedly and incessantly about Jesus.

Initially, the stories were firsthand verbal testimonies: A person whose health had been restored by Jesus. A neighbor who had been there when Jesus argued with the religious leaders at the temple. A woman with a story about seeing Jesus alive after his crucifixion and burial.

The Christian Gospels began—similar to the books of the Hebrew Bible—as oral traditions. Jesus said and did certain things. People watched and listened, then shared anecdotes. They told what they had seen or experienced. Disciples repeated the *parables* (stories used to teach moral principles) and teachings of Jesus. At some later point—nobody knows exactly when—others began to write down these things. Traditionally, Christianity has believed that the apostles for whom the Gospels are named were their actual authors. Most modern academic scholars believe that these Gospels were written later and attributed to the apostles or associates of the apostles.

It is worth noting that Matthew—one of Jesus's twelve apostles and, in the eyes of many, the author of the Gospel that bears his name—was a tax collector by trade. This meant he could and did write. It means that, like others in his trade, he probably knew and used a kind of shorthand. Is it possible that Matthew might have functioned as an unofficial secretary for Jesus, or at least jotted down notes, keeping records of various experiences? The idea cannot be proven, but it is not far-fetched.

We know this: the author of the third New Testament Gospel begins his written portrait of Jesus with this admission:

> Since many have undertaken to set down an orderly account of the events that have been fulfilled among us, just as they were handed on to us by those who from the beginning were eyewitnesses and servants of the word, I too decided, after investigating everything carefully from the very first, to write an orderly account for you, most excellent Theophilus, so that you may know the truth concerning the things about which you have been instructed. (Luke 1:1–4)

The claim here is that Luke drew upon other sources. He investigated "everything carefully." Like a good researcher, he almost certainly conducted interviews with eyewitnesses. (He was, after all, a colleague of the apostle Paul, who also worked with Mark, who was associated with Peter). And this introduction seems to refer to written accounts that "were handed on to us by those who from the beginning were eyewitnesses."

Some scholars speculate that perhaps early on (in the 30s or 40s CE) someone began compiling a comprehensive collection of the words and works of Jesus. Less an organized work and more a file of information, this is often referred to as the Q document (from the German word *Quelle*, which means "source"). It's an intriguing and plausible theory; however, no such document has ever been found.

As these Gospel accounts were written, they began to circulate among Jesus's followers—apparently much more quickly than scholars once believed.

One evidence of this is the famous Rylands P52 manuscript fragment. This tattered scrap of papyrus—no more than 2.5 by 3.5 inches—features, on front and back, a few verses from the eighteenth chapter of the Gospel of John. It was obtained in 1920 in Egypt by Bernard P. Grenfell, professor of papyrology at Oxford. It sat unnoticed for more than a decade in a stack of manuscript fragments at the John Rylands Library in Manchester, England. However, in 1934, C. H. Roberts, a publisher at Oxford University Press, came across the fragment and recognized it as a very old copy of John's Gospel. Upon further review, he realized, based on the style of its script, that P52 likely originated in the first half of the second century.

If so, then in a relatively short period of time, we have a Gospel being written—tradition says in Ephesus (modern-day Turkey)—then copied and carried to North Africa, potentially within a decade of the writing of the original. This is exactly what we would expect for any document perceived as containing "good news."

We get another peek into the circulation of the Christian Gospels in the writings of Justin Martyr, a second-century philosopher and defender of the Christian faith. In his work entitled *First Apology*, Justin describes worship services among Christians in Rome around 150 CE:

> On the day called Sunday, all who live in cities or in the country gather together to one place, and the memoirs of the apostles or the writings of the prophets are read, as long as time permits; then, when the reader has ceased, the president [church leader] verbally instructs, and exhorts to the imitation of these good things. Then we all rise together and pray.[3]

"The memoirs of the apostles" is how early Christians sometimes referred to the Gospels. Notice that already by 150 CE, these written accounts of the life of Jesus were viewed by Christians as being on par with the writings of the Hebrew prophets.

As the Nag Hammadi discovery showed, Matthew, Mark, Luke, and John weren't the only Gospels circulating in the second through fourth centuries. It seems that everyone was weighing in on the life of Jesus, claiming to reveal never-before-heard stories and teachings.

Many of these texts include eyebrow-raising claims. For example, the Infancy Gospel of Thomas includes a passage describing Jesus, as a young boy, making clay birds come to life and fly away. A section in the Gospel of Philip purportedly reads, "The companion of the [Savior is] Mary Magdalene. [But Christ loved] her more than [all] the disciples, and used to kiss her [often] on her [mouth]. The rest of [the disciples were offended] . . . They said to him, 'Why do you love her more than all of us?' The Savior answered and said to them, 'Why do I not love you as [I love] her?'"

Author Dan Brown seized on this mysterious fragment and its incomplete statement (notice all the brackets where scholars had to supply their own words because of damage to the manuscript) to concoct an entertaining, provocative story about the Catholic Church attempting to cover up the fact that Jesus and Mary Magdalene were husband and wife and had a child together. Brown's novel, *The Da Vinci Code*, released in 2003, was marketed as a mystery suspense thriller rooted in hidden, historical fact. It found a wide audience. In six years, it sold eighty million copies worldwide. Most agree that it is an engaging story; few scholars put much credence in its "historical" claims.

In 2012, Harvard Divinity School professor Karen L. King rocked the religious and academic worlds when she announced the discovery of an ancient Coptic fragment that read: "Jesus said to them, 'My wife.'" Some saw in this announcement a validation of Dan Brown's fictional *Da Vinci Code* plot. At the very least it seemed to reinforce Pagels's questioning why certain Gospels were quickly discounted and considered unworthy of scriptural status. After all, couldn't the Gnostic Gospels contain hidden truths about early Christianity?

In 2014, Christian Askeland, a Coptic specialist, determined that this so-called Gospel of Jesus' Wife matched another papyrus fragment that was clearly forged. One of the editors of this book broke the story in the *Wall Street Journal*, in an article titled "How the Jesus' Wife Hoax Fell Apart."[4] However, a major TV documentary aired a couple of days later highlighting the forgery as an alleged discovery. Dr. King continued to defend the authenticity of the document until an investigative report by *The Atlantic* uncovered very damning evidence to the contrary. In June 2016, Dr. King finally admitted to the magazine that the papyrus is most likely a forgery.

The Gospel of Jesus' Wife is a sobering reminder—a cautionary tale—that not every Gospel is "gospel truth."

CHAPTER SIX

HATRED AND HERETICS

Assembling the New Testament

When you come, bring the cloak that
I left with Carpus at Troas,
also the books, and above all the parchments.

—The apostle Paul (2 Timothy 4:13)

He could sense it. He could read it in the body language of his captors. Even the prison's burliest, surliest guard had stopped making eye contact.

Whether in a few days or a matter of weeks, Paul would be ushered from his cell—and *not* to appear before a Roman magistrate.

This time around there would be no hearings—and certainly no release. There would be no future travels to far-flung places for Paul to share his belief that Jesus was the promised Messiah. He would never again feel the adrenaline rush of standing in front of an angry mob or the joy of speaking to a receptive audience.

The signs were everywhere. Not just his life's work but his life itself was coming to an end. Paul's next appointment would be with an executioner. The old apostle had always suspected things would end this way, even if a big part of him always hoped they wouldn't.

Paul was never one, however, to mope or fret or waste an opportunity. Ever committed to the notion of "making the most of the time" (Ephesians 5:16), he decided to send one last letter. It would be a final missive to his young protégé, Timothy, who was leading a congregation of Christians in Ephesus. It is the letter that the Christian Bible calls 2 Timothy.

Of the New Testament's twenty-seven writings, almost half are the correspondence of Paul. (While traditional Christianity considers all these to be written by Paul, many critical scholars see some of these as written by Paul's followers after his death.) Second Timothy, traditionally dated to 66–67 CE, is seen by those who accept its Pauline authorship as Paul's most personal letter. (The critical scholars we have mentioned, however, see this as dating to late in the first century.) In any case, this letter provides us a valuable glimpse into a tumultuous period of history when the Christian church was growing, suffering, and hammering out its beliefs.

The final few centuries leading up to the Common Era were crucial for the formation of the Hebrew Bible. Likewise, the first few centuries of the Common Era were pivotal for the formation of the New Testament.

Second Timothy presents itself as Paul's last will and testament, and it contains multiple references to opposition to the Christians and their message in the mid-to-late first century. The author said emphatically, "All who want to live a godly life in Christ Jesus will be persecuted" (2 Timothy 3:12). This sobering statement sounds an awful lot like a guarantee—though it's not exactly the kind of spiritual promise that people of faith like to cross-stitch, frame, and hang above the living room sofa.

Paul made it clear that he wasn't exempt from this grim reality. "I suffer hardship, even to the point of being chained like a criminal" (2:9). Yet not once in this brief communiqué did he coach his young charge to seek to avoid a similar fate. On the contrary, he urged, "Join with me in suffering for the gospel" (1:8). And just in case Timothy might have somehow missed his point, Paul added a final challenge to "endure suffering" (4:5). Clearly, it wasn't easy or safe being a Christian in the Roman Empire in 66 CE. In many parts of the world today, that is still true.

Paul repeatedly warned Timothy to guard against theological error. "Hold to the standard of sound teaching that you have heard from me" (1:13), he exhorted. Keep an eye out for teachers "who have swerved from the truth" (2:18) and who "oppose the truth" (3:8), he cautioned. In short, he called his younger associate to cling to God-inspired "scripture" (3:15–16). And don't just embrace it personally, he admonished; "proclaim the message" to others (4:2).

Why so much emphasis on "the sacred writings" (3:15)? Paul gives the reason as he draws his thoughts to a close: "For the time is coming when people will not put up with sound doctrine, but having itching ears, they will accumulate for themselves teachers to suit their own desires, and will turn away from listening to the truth and wander away to myths" (4:3–4).

Here in Paul's final letter is evidence of two fundamental and powerful realities at work during the era in which the New Testament was being composed and consolidated: persecution from outside the church and problems within the church.

What do we know, really, about the beginnings of the Christian faith? Following the four Gospels that document the life of Jesus, the New Testament gives us the book of Acts. This brief history documents key events in the first three or so decades of the early church. The Pentecost event, described in Acts 2, shows the apostles Peter and John leading the young Jesus movement. Like a giant rock dropped into a pond, the gospel is shown making a tremendous splash at Jerusalem—or creating waves, depending on one's point of view. This much is true: Upon hearing the message of Jesus, few people were neutral. Most either vehemently rejected or enthusiastically embraced it.

When the rejection became deadly (see the stoning of Stephen in Acts 8), many of these new Christians fled Jerusalem. Like ripples, they spread outward in every direction. As they did, they took the gospel message with them, and they kept sharing it with others.

Acts 9 tells the story of how the church's fiercest enemy became its foremost ambassador. Saul was converted, probably in 33–34 CE, and became known as Paul. Within a decade, he seems to be regarded by most of the Christian community as an apostle. The book of Acts shows him engaged in vigorous missionary activity with a simple strategy: Every time he entered a city, Paul went first to the nearest synagogue. There, according to the book of Acts, he tried to persuade his Jewish brethren that Jesus was the Messiah foretold in the Tanakh.

Next, he would speak about Jesus to Gentiles. If he had any spiritually receptive people in either audience—and assuming he didn't get attacked, arrested, or run out of town—he would stick around long enough to band these new believers into a local church. Time permitting, he would teach them as much of the existing Bible (the Hebrew Scriptures) as possible before heading to the next town. In each of his New Testament letters, Paul (who lived during the reigns of Caligula, Claudius, and Nero, three of history's most notorious anti-Christian emperors), spoke matter-of-factly about his frequent mistreatment (see 2 Corinthians 11:23–28 for the most complete list of his sufferings).

Persecution wasn't reserved for leaders like Paul. It was a way of life for most Christians in the first three centuries of the Common Era.

The persecution of Christians is documented in classical literature. Tacitus, a Roman historian, wrote about how Christians were despised in first-century Roman culture. Another historian, Suetonius, confirmed the expulsion of Jews and Jewish-Christians from Rome, likely between 49 and 52 CE.

From the time of Caligula in 37 CE, through the reign of Diocletian in 305 CE, Christians were an easy and frequent scapegoat. Tertullian, a leader in the early church, put it this way in his *Apology*: "If the Tiber floods the city, or if the Nile refuses to rise, or if the sky withholds its rain, if there is an earthquake, a famine, a pestilence, at once the cry is raised, 'Christians to the lions.'" Consequently, over those two and a half centuries, at least ten wide-scale, government-sanctioned persecutions broke out against the church.

Diocletian's hatred of the Christian faith was especially intense. He not only wanted to kill Christian believers, but he also sought to eradicate every vestige of the Christian faith. He had gathering places destroyed. He ordered the burning of all sacred Scriptures. The brutal nature of his reign is captured in the English Protestant classic, *Foxe's Book of Martyrs*.[1] This book, though controversial and reliant more on anecdotal evidence than definitive historical sources, nevertheless gives a general sense of how early Christians were often treated.

For example, in 304, a newlywed North African church leader named Timothy was "carried before Arrianus, the governor of

Thebais [Thebes], who, knowing that he had the keeping of [the responsibility for maintaining] the Holy Scriptures, commanded him to deliver them up to be burnt; to which he answered, 'Had I children, I would sooner deliver them up to be sacrificed, than part with the Word of God.' The governor being much incensed at this reply, ordered his eyes to be put out with red-hot irons, saying 'The books shall at least be useless to you, for you shall not see to read them.'" Shortly after, Timothy and his bride of less than three weeks were crucified.[2]

We also have examples of similar inhumane treatment of followers of the Hebrew Bible. Rabbinic texts preserve various accounts of martyrdom at the hands of the Romans in the aftermath of the great revolt of the Jews against Rome (66–73 CE) and the Bar Kokhba Revolt (132–135 CE). One of the most well-known is the martyrdom of Rabbi Akiva, the leading sage of his generation. Rabbi Akiva publicly disobeyed the Roman prohibition of the teaching of Torah. The Romans arrested him, then flayed his flesh with iron combs. Despite the pain, he recited the *Shema*, declaring God's unity and sovereignty, accepting the opportunity to sanctify God's name with his life. According to Jewish tradition, when he reached the word "one," proclaiming his monotheistic belief, his soul departed.

So, the first three centuries of Christianity were marked by continual, often intense persecution. The church didn't get a respite until Constantine become emperor in 313 CE. But attacks from without weren't the church's only problem. The church also had to deal with spiritual confusion that likely prompted many of the New Testament epistles (letters). The apostles began corresponding with congregations and church leaders—answering a host of spiritual questions and weighing in on a number of fierce theological debates, many of which revolved around the nature of Jesus.

Thus, over the final half of the first century, in addition to the accepted Jewish Scriptures (the Tanakh, or Hebrew Bible), a number of newer writings began to circulate among the churches.

There were the Gospel records from Matthew, Mark, Luke, and John, explaining who Jesus was and what he said and did. There was the book of Acts, Luke's carefully researched history of the early church, highlighting key events through approximately 60–61 CE. There were twenty-one pieces of epistolary literature (letters attributed almost entirely to Paul, John, Peter, and James). Some of these letters contained broad theological teaching; others gave practical instructions for personal piety and corporate worship. Finally, there was the cryptic book of Revelation, an apocalyptic prophecy traditionally attributed to the apostle John.

By about 100 CE or soon after, all twenty-seven books of what is now known as the New Testament had been written and sent by apostles to congregations or church leaders. But in a primitive era with no copying machines, no FedEx, and no Internet, these writings were scattered over much of the Roman Empire and to the East as well. It would be years, decades even, before Christian communities in other parts of the world had copies of all the writings included in the New Testament canon.

Early copies also began appearing in other languages, with perhaps the earliest being a harmony of the Gospels in Syriac, by Tatian around 170 CE, known as the Diatessaron. Two partial copies of an Old Syriac Version of the Gospels from the fifth century CE survive, as well as a Peshitta (or "simple" and without textual comments) version of much of the Old and New Testaments, also from the fifth century. Around 350 manuscript copies of the Peshitta exist.

Around the same time the Peshitta first appeared, various Coptic Old and New Testament manuscripts were being copied in Egypt, indicating likely translations from the Greek in the third century CE. We saw earlier that some Coptic manuscripts from Nag Hammadi created sensational interest. Some of the Nag Hammadi texts built on earlier copies of the Bible. Besides Greek copies of the New Testament, known in large part from discarded materials from the Oxyrhynchus dump site, these Egyptians also had various copies in Coptic. Some of the most recognized ones today, because of their early dates and state of preservation, are the Bodmer Papyri (named for Martin Bodmer, who purchased them). These were found in 1952 not far from the Nag Hammadi site, and many were taken to Switzerland and the Chester Beatty Library. A dozen are in Coptic. Recently, important sections were sold to the Vatican Library and to the Green Collection, housed at Museum of the Bible in Washington, DC. The glass insert inside forty-foot bronze doors of the Museum of the Bible contain an etched image of one of these leaves (Greek of Psalms).

By that time—certainly by the second and third centuries—there were numerous *other* writings making the rounds as well. The previously mentioned Gnostic Gospels were circulating, along with a set of Infancy Gospels (focusing on the childhood of Jesus), Jewish-Christian Gospels (cited by later church leaders such as Clement and Origen), and Passion Gospels (concentrating on the crucifixion and resurrection of Jesus). There were numerous histories—similar to the book of Acts, only connected to individual apostles and leaders of the early church. There were lots of other popular epistles—attributed to leaders like Barnabas, Clement, and Ignatius—read and treasured by Christians across the Roman Empire. Finally, there was a batch of apocalyptic literature—like the Revelation of John, but ascribed to other church leaders like Peter, Paul, James, Stephen, and the Shepherd of Hermas. They varied in their style and in their agreement with the earlier Gospels and letters now comprising the New Testament.

This ever-growing collection of new and varied writings prompted all sorts of questions among the faithful: Are all these religious texts equally valid? Was Jesus human or divine? What is the connection, if any, between Judaism and Christianity? What are the defining beliefs and distinctive behaviors of a Christian?

In certain ways, not much has changed in 1,900 years. People in the second century embraced conflicting ideas, opinions, and beliefs about spirituality, just as people in the twenty-first century do. If you Google the word "God," you will get more than 1.5 billion results! Rest assured, not all those webpages and blog posts and articles say the same thing.

It took a man with shocking ideas to get the early church to draw some biblical boundaries and reach some important theological conclusions.

Marcion was from Sinope, Turkey. Historians tell us that he was the son of a bishop who made a fortune in the ship-building business.

Though he wasn't a clergyman, Marcion had a strong interest in religious matters, and he gave generously to the church. Yet as he studied the Christian Gospels and Epistles alongside the Hebrew Bible, he decided the two sets of writings were incompatible. He concluded it was impossible to reconcile the God of the Old Testament with the person of Jesus of Nazareth.

So Marcion proposed a novel religious idea. He decided there must be two gods—one, the lesser, vengeful, tribal deity of the Jews; the other, the greater, loving transcendent God and Father of Jesus. Not only that, but Marcion expressed his belief that Jesus had been truly divine, but not truly human. He only *seemed* to have a physical body.

For this new belief system, Marcion designed his own "Bible." He threw out the entire Old Testament and any Christian writings that undermined his conclusions. Considering that the New Testament is replete with references to the Old Testament, including from Jesus himself, the result was a very short list of sacred books: Luke's Gospel (minus the first two chapters about the physical birth of Jesus) and ten of Paul's thirteen letters.

When Marcion's views began to gain traction, church leaders stepped in. They labeled his ideas as heresy (beliefs considered far out of the mainstream) and began the process of excommunicating him. The conflict got heated and extremely personal. At one point, Polycarp, the Christian bishop of Smyrna, Turkey, called Marcion "the firstborn of Satan." After Marcion, spiritual leaders from all over began weighing in on which writings were canonical—and which ones were not. Before long, many people were suggesting lists.

We have said that the Greek word *canon* means "measuring stick" or "ruler." Applied to ancient religious writings, this word came to refer to the collection of books that are seen as inspired by God and authoritative as a rule for life. Thus, people speak of "the canon of Scripture." *Canonical* books are books that "measure up" to the standard of sacred Scripture.

It's important to clarify that *canonicity* is more than an arbitrary designation bestowed on a writing by a group of religious leaders meeting in a room somewhere. It is a recognition by a wide audience that a work shows signs of being inspired.

So, what were the criteria by which certain ancient writings were deemed to be canonical by the Christian church—and others were not?

The early church looked for certain factors. Although they didn't use a specific checklist, it seems that at least five tests, administered in no particular order, helped guide ancient believers in recognizing twenty-seven first-century writings—and no others—as being canonical:

- *The Relational Test.* A work had to be connected to a known and revered leader of the church. If a writing could not be established as the work of an apostle (or at least a close associate of an apostle), then it was discounted.
- *The Chronological Test.* Writings that didn't materialize until the second or third centuries (or later)—after the first-generation apostles were long gone—were viewed with suspicion.
- *The Doctrinal Test.* For a document to be regarded as Scripture, its teaching had to be consistent with the accepted teachings of Jesus and the apostles.
- *The Practical Test.* A writing, to be warranted as divinely inspired, had to show itself to be universally helpful to readers and conducive to spiritual life and growth.
- *The Spiritual Test.* Jews and Christians see in their holy writings a supernatural quality—a divine power or sacred gravitas,

if you will. Some Christians today use the term "the witness of the Spirit" to speak of a deep, internal sense that a particular writing isn't merely good to read but inspired by God.

With this very loose list of tests, the early church set out to reach consensus on which books should be added to the Hebrew Scriptures. The process would not be quick or easy.

Humans love lists. "Here are the six things I need to do today." "Here are the three best pizza joints in town." "Here are the AP's top twenty-five football teams." "Here are ten commandments God wants his people to follow."

Lists are our attempts to simplify and clarify. By them we include and exclude. After Marcion produced his short list of acceptable Scriptures in the mid-second century, other prominent leaders came forward with their own.

A later manuscript preserves a text dated by scholars to between 170 and 200 CE that includes a list that refers to the gospel of Luke and includes twenty-two of the twenty-seven books that are now considered as the New Testament canon. (It does, however, list the Revelation of Peter in addition to the Revelation of John.) This manuscript fragment was found in 1740 in an Italian library by a historian named Muratori—thus its name, the Muratorian Fragment. This translated copy is regarded as representing the oldest known list of New Testament books. At the very least, it suggests that the core of the New Testament canon was already established by this time.

Irenaeus (130–202 CE) was a bishop in France who famously defended the church against unorthodox ideas. In his famous work *Against Heresies*, he quoted from Christian writings he considered Scripture. Of the current books of the New Testament, Philemon, 2 Peter, 3 John, and Jude are the only books he does not cite.

Not long after that, witty author and fiery theologian Tertullian (160–220 CE) listed the writings he viewed as divinely inspired. He included the epistle of Jude, and—like Irenaeus—referenced the Shepherd of Hermas (though he later changed his mind about the Shepherd of Hermas as Scripture).

Origen (185–254 CE) was another influential scholar and philosopher during this era. He is probably best remembered for his ascetic practices. He fasted regularly, refused to wear shoes, and reportedly castrated himself so that his desire might be for God alone! Epiphanius (ca. 320–403 CE) attacked some of Origen's central views as unorthodox, but in the process, he commented on Origen's prolific nature. In what may be hyperbole, he claimed that Origen produced some 6,000 works. Few have survived, and many were short (one page or so), but among the ones that we have is his list of *accepted* Scriptures (books widely regarded as sacred) and *disputed* books (such as James, 2 and 3 John, Jude, 2 Peter, the Shepherd of Hermas, and the Letter of Barnabas).

The year 325 CE produced a milestone moment in the creation of the New Testament. The Roman emperor Constantine—the first Roman emperor to profess Christianity—convened the Council of

Nicaea to discuss theological issues. Attending this conference was Eusebius, a prominent bishop from Caesarea. There at Nicaea this "father of church history" interacted with Christian leaders from all over the known world. In effect, he surveyed them to learn what Christian writings were regarded as Scripture in their locales.

The following year (326 CE), Eusebius published his magnum opus, *Ecclesiastical History*, in which he noted there was no universal consensus on which Christian writings constitute Scripture. He did, however, offer his own list—with the caveat that some of the books he regarded as canonical (James, 2 Peter, John's epistles, Jude, and Revelation) were still disputed by some church leaders. It is worth noting that Eusebius's list is the same as the New Testament in use today.

One other fact and one other name from this era are worth knowing.

The fact to remember is Emperor Constantine's 331 CE order for fifty copies of the Bible in Greek. Just three decades earlier, the former Roman emperor, Diocletian, called for the destruction of Christian Scriptures. Now Constantine was calling for their production! No one can say for sure, but some believe that Codex Sinaiticus, discovered in Egypt by another Constantin (i.e., Tischendorf, see chapter 1), was one of those fifty copies. It is, after all, the oldest complete copy of the New Testament.

The name to remember is Athanasius (296–373 CE), the Egyptian bishop of Alexandria. His blunt, feisty personality got him exiled multiple times by different Roman emperors. But the upside of all this "mandated travel" was that Athanasius became familiar with Christian views of Scripture throughout the empire. In 367 CE, he wrote an Easter letter in which he urged the churches under his care to read Scripture in worship. In this letter, Athanasius mentioned the same twenty-seven New Testament books recognized by most mainstream Christians today.

After enduring some 300 years of hatred and heresy, the church had finally agreed on a canon of Scripture to guide them into the future.

However, even as Christians were settling on a Greek Bible with agreed-upon Old and New Testaments, Jewish scholars were continuing to transmit the Hebrew Bible—and one scholar was preparing a definitive edition of the Bible in Latin.

CHAPTER SEVEN

THE MASORETES AND JEROME

Standardizing Scripture

Oh, reader, take note. While the hand that copied this text molders in the grave . . . the Word copied lives forever!

—An anonymous medieval scribe

What kid (for that matter, what adult) doesn't smile at the thought of finding hidden treasure?

You may remember the Pennsylvania man who bought a flea-market painting in 1989 because he liked the frame, only to find folded up behind the painting one of the twenty-four original, official copies of the Declaration of Independence. His $4 purchase netted him $2.42 million at auction!

Or maybe you heard about the California man who in 2011 paid $1,100 for the contents of an abandoned storage unit . . . then discovered $500,000 worth of gold and silver bars and rare coins inside a blue Rubbermaid container.

You probably haven't heard about the two Florida doctors in 1972 who bought some Hebrew scroll fragments from an antiquities dealer in Beirut, only to learn they were of inestimable historic value.

Dr. Fuad Ashkar, a specialist in nuclear medicine and radiology, and his wife, Theresa, began buying ancient artifacts in 1960. By the 1970s, the couple had amassed a personal collection worth more than a million dollars.

While in Lebanon in 1972, Ashkar visited a broker named Taha Nassar, who showed him a collection of old Torah fragments. Their origin was unknown, though some experts have since speculated they were likely part of the famous Cairo Genizah discovery of 1896 (see chapter 12).

The manuscripts, of various sizes and shapes, were written in Hebrew on parchment and were in reasonably good condition. Nassar expressed his opinion that the documents probably dated from the second to the tenth centuries CE. Ashkar consulted with his father, a professor of ancient languages at the Lebanese

University in Beirut, then paid Nassar $1,000 for two of the sixty fragments.

Upon returning to Miami, Ashkar showed his new acquisitions to a colleague, Dr. Albert Gilson. Agreeing that the documents seemed very rare and extremely valuable, the men decided to buy twenty additional pieces from Nassar for $10,000. Later that year, the men attempted to buy the remaining thirty-eight fragments of Nassar's collection, but they were too late. He had already sold them to some German investors.

In 1976, Anwar Bikhazi, a Lebanese doctor, approached the men and offered the American equivalent of $250,000 for their twenty-two-fragment collection. They declined. Two years later, Dr. Bikhazi upped his offer to more than $335,000. Again, Ashkar and Gilson refused to sell.

It was late 1977 by the time Theresa Ashkar heard of the work of Dr. James Charlesworth, director of graduate studies in New Testament and ancient Judaism at Duke University. She contacted him to discuss the fragment collection she and her husband co-owned with Gilson. Charlesworth perked up immediately. He had several discussions with the doctors about the documents and became more intrigued. The following year (1978), when invited to fly to Miami to examine the documents, Dr. Charlesworth caught the first plane south.

Long story short, the doctors allowed Charlesworth to take the fragments to Duke University for further analysis. Then, over the next three years (1979–1981), the doctors ended up donating the entire collection to the university. The value of the fragments—at least according to the Internal Revenue Service—was set at $337,500.

Yet their worth is much greater than a nice tax deduction.

The Dead Sea Scrolls (see chapter 4), gave the world exquisite biblical texts from 200 BCE, and the famous Aleppo Codex (see chapter 8) gave the world a priceless Bible from the early tenth century CE. But what about all those years in between?

Analysis of the Ashkar-Gilson fragments shed new light on how the Hebrew Bible was transmitted in the centuries following the destruction of the Jerusalem temple in 70 CE.

Scholars at Duke authenticated all twenty-two fragments as being part of an ancient Torah scroll. They include text from all five books of the Pentateuch, plus a portion of the Jewish Yom Kippur liturgy. Using carbon-14 dating methods, researchers concluded that the scroll had been written between 600 and 980 CE.

This fact makes the Ashkar-Gilson Hebrew Manuscript the oldest known Hebrew version of Exodus 15. (Exodus 15 is a national song of celebration that followed the Israelites' Red Sea crossing and is thus referred to the "Song of the Sea.")

In 2007, Duke University loaned the largest fragment (#2) to the Israel Museum, who put it on display at the Shrine of the Book. There, it caught the eye of two Jewish scholars, Dr. Mordechay Mishor and Dr. Edna Engel, who suspected the manuscript was from the same Torah scroll as the well-known London manuscript. Further study confirmed their hunch.

Until the Ashkar-Gilson collection surfaced, we had almost no Hebrew manuscripts from the third to eighth centuries CE. Thanks to a little antiquities shopping and investing, two doctors from Florida helped bridge that gap. Some have even gone so far as to call their donated manuscript the "missing link" in Hebrew Bible research.[1]

A second group was also at work during that era—helping people understand the Bible.

The Old Testament teaches that God gave Moses the *written* Torah at Sinai. Christians and Jews share this belief. However, Jews believe that at the same time Moses was also given an *oral* Torah (the spoken explanation for how to interpret and carry out the written laws).

The written Torah was, as its name suggests, written down. The oral Torah was not. This arrangement was to ensure that the law could be properly applied to the many complicated circumstances Jews would face and that the Torah could be observed in changing times and environments. The oral Torah was passed down from one generation to the next, older sages imparting timeless truth to up-and-coming teachers.

As long as the Jewish people had a homeland, a centralized temple, and a clearly defined leadership structure (the Sanhedrin, a kind of high court containing a variety of rabbis and functioning as a judicial and legislative body), this system worked perfectly. But with the Roman destruction of the Second Temple in 70 CE, followed by waves of persecution, the rabbis and sages of the Jewish people were often persecuted and sometimes went into hiding. Some underwent martyrdom when the Romans forbade the study and teaching of the Torah. Jews fled the land of Israel in large numbers after the two failed Jewish revolts against Rome in 66–73 CE and 132–35 CE. Others fled Byzantine Christian persecutions in the fourth through sixth centuries. Without a way to pass on the collective wisdom of the rabbis, it was feared that the Jewish people might forget the oral law.

Enter Rabbi Yehudah HaNasi ("Judah, the Prince"). Often called Rebbe in traditional Jewish circles, Yehudah was a brilliant scholar and charismatic leader who, according to many scholars, was able to befriend Roman emperor Marcus Aurelius (161–180 CE). Though conditions for Jews improved briefly as a result, uncertainty loomed. This prompted Rabbi Yehudah to begin the monumental effort of compiling, editing, and summarizing *all* the Torah's legal and ritual interpretations, principles, and teachings, together with the rulings of the great Jewish rabbis through the centuries. He even crafted an important ethical summary known as Ethics of the Fathers. The result of his efforts was a massive, amazing collection called the *Mishnah* (which means "repetition" or "recitation"). Some believe Yehudah did all this orally. Others are convinced he committed all this to writing between 170–200 CE.

Oral or written, this is when and how the Mishnah came into existence. The idea was that a Jew—even if living far from Israel and not having access to rabbinical teaching—could learn the way of God by continually studying and reviewing this concise summary of the oral law.

Although Jewish communities began using various other languages in or around Judea, such as Greek and Aramaic (and then various others during their diasporas), the Mishnah was written in Hebrew—the language of Jewish religious study and teaching. The Mishnah was a major force in ensuring that future generations might not lose or forget the language of their forefathers, as so many had done during the time of the Babylonian exile and following.

During the next couple of centuries, more and more Jews—including more and more rabbis—left Israel, many for Babylonia (a region in present-day Iraq). This dispersion further weakened rabbinical authority and consensus in the land of Israel but helped the sages of Babylonia who would carry on and greatly enrich the Jewish oral tradition.

It was decided that Rabbi Yehudah's Mishnah was too concise and needed to be fleshed out in more detail. Further, biblical sources had to be explored and contradictions with other traditions had to be reconciled. The result was the more comprehensive *Talmud* (which means "instruction" or "learning"). Jews see the Talmud as the primary text of rabbinic Judaism.

Actually, two Talmuds emerged—an unfinished one put together by the rabbis in Israel, known as the Jerusalem Talmud, and a more authoritative one by those living in Babylonia, known as the Babylonian Talmud. The Jerusalem Talmud was compiled in the beginning of the fifth century; the Babylonian Talmud from the sixth century through the Muslim conquest (ca. 640 CE). Editing and correction of the text of both continued long after these dates.

A veritable encyclopedia of Jewish law, life, and history, the Talmud contains the Mishnah—the oral law—as explained and codified by rabbis who lived from around 30 BCE to 200 CE. It also contains the *Gemara*—later commentaries on and interpretations of the Mishnah—as well as numerous other theological, ethical, legal, and ritual teachings by rabbis from roughly 200 to 500 CE.

The rabbis saw the written Torah and the rest of the Hebrew Bible as the authoritative bedrock of Judaism. They believed the written law was mediated and complemented by the oral law. On the solid foundation of the written law, the oral law provided the conceptual and structural framework for Jewish ethics, belief, and ritual. Together, one might say the written and oral law formed a sort of portable sanctuary in which a Jewish man or woman could live and worship God anywhere on earth.

As you might guess, the Talmud is massive. One version for sale online is 30 volumes and has more than 15,000 pages! Another has a shipping weight of 342 pounds.

Some admit that reading the Talmud feels, at times, like listening to a lively debate among a group of highly opinionated rabbis. To the uninformed onlooker these intense discussions can sometimes seem like a lot of semantic hair-splitting. But the goal is not arguing; it is aligning one's life to eternal truth.

If the rabbis worked to help Jewish people everywhere understand Scripture, then the Masoretes of the early Middle Ages worked so that Jewish people everywhere might have the same Scripture. The Masoretes undertook a very difficult responsibility: trying to standardize the reading and cantillation (the way it was meant to be chanted during ritual worship) of the biblical text. Textual variation is probably as old as the Bible itself. Ancient copyists often made errors or introduced small modifications into texts they copied. Further, sometimes varying editions of the very same text circulated, as is the case as Jeremiah's scribe tells us that he was instructed to rewrite his work, a kind of second edition. This can also be seen by comparing Samuel and Kings with their reflection in parallel passages in Chronicles.

But in the case of Israel's Scriptures, historical factors also took their toll. In 722 BCE, the collapse of the Northern Kingdom of Israel led to the exile of Israelites to northern Mesopotamia. Later, when the First Temple era was brought to a close by the destruction of the First Temple, many citizens of Judea went into Babylonian captivity (597 and 586 BCE), and Judaism became geographically even more decentralized. Though the Babylonian exile lasted only a few decades, it contributed to a steady dispersion of the Jewish people (and holy scrolls) to disparate places.

Even when they were finally given the chance to return to the land of their forefathers, many Jewish exiles elected to remain in their new homes. For those who did return to the land of Israel, Second Temple biblical manuscripts preserved in the Dead Sea Scrolls indicate that substantial variation existed in these texts and that there were different families of texts. The process of standardization was undertaken by the Pharisees and rabbis, and examination of the first-century scrolls at Masada and other sites in the Judean Desert shows evidence of this standardization.

Later, the Greco-Roman Diaspora led Jews to many new destinations. In time, Jews could be found from Babylonia to Iran, as far north as Afghanistan and in Yemen to the south, and westward into southern Europe and North Africa. In each of these distant places, small changes began to creep into the biblical texts as they were copied and passed on. Before long, the Bible passages being read by Jews in Palestine, Asia Minor, Egypt, Persia, and Arabia began to diverge from one another, as did the traditions regarding matters of pronunciation and cantillation.

The wonderful thing about the advance of scholarship is that we can track most of these changes, and in many cases, we can even determine whether they were using the same exemplar (an earlier text from which copies are made). This has become a major focus in critical textual studies. Scholars in the United States, Canada, Europe and Israel, in secular and religious universities, and in seminaries, both Jewish and Christian, study the transmission and history of the biblical text in the various ancient languages, preparing editions and textual studies. Academic and interreligious cooperation is a key to the success of this research. The Museum of the Bible Scholars Initiative involves scholars from nearly 100 institutions working on biblical and other ancient texts in its collections.

It's a rare writer anymore who uses pen and paper (much less reed pens and papyrus). Most modern authors compose documents electronically. This book you are reading, for example, was written using Microsoft Word and involved scholars and editors from several US states and a few countries. This team was able to interact seamlessly because of the features of this software, including one that enables them to track changes in a document. It's a remarkably helpful tool. Editors can insert words or delete sentences, then e-mail the document back and forth. What's more, each reviewer can be assigned a different color, so it's possible to see which person made which comments or edits—and all with time stamps.

The beauty of such technology is that at the click of a button, one can see the latest version of the document. Or one can also, with a click of a button, go back to the original version of the document.

Tracking the scribal changes in documents written and copied by hand in various places over centuries is much more laborious. Ancient parchments don't come with color-coding to highlight changes. Almost like detectives on a crime scene, biblical scholars have to pore over manuscript evidence. When various documents say different things, textual experts have to ask questions, piece together tricky timelines, and rely on forensics and logic to determine which document came first and to ascertain which witnesses are reliable and which ones are suspect. The job is made tougher because many ancient documents are missing sections due to wear and tear.

In the Second Temple period (516 BCE–70 CE), this is what the priests, and later, the Pharisaic-rabbinical sages set out to do in fixing the consonantal text of Scripture. When looking at texts with variant readings (almost always scrolls), they tried to solve the mystery of which reading was closer to the original and therefore more accurate. They tried to dismiss inaccurate manuscript witnesses and find the truthful ones.

They were standardizing the Bible.

When the Masoretes emerged around the sixth or seventh century, the project got serious. Really serious. For several hundred intense years.

Who were the Masoretes? The Hebrew word Masorah refers to the Jewish tradition of handing down holy texts and ensuring that such documents are transmitted correctly. Thus, the Masoretes were like a school of scholarly scribes. They were like ancient PhDs in Hebrew Bible. They were the original transmission experts. They knew how the biblical text was supposed to be pronounced when it was read. They also knew its proper cantillation.

The largest and most famous group of Masoretes were members of the Ben Asher family. They lived and worked primarily in Tiberias (a city in northern Israel). Other Masoretes were based in Babylonia (a region near present-day Iraq).

The Masoretes' mission was simple, though not easy to accomplish: create a full, final, accurate, and standardized version of the Bible. And not just some arbitrary version, but the version given by God.

Hebrew is a beautiful but strange language (at least to most non-Hebrew-speakers). The alphabet consists of no vowels and 22 consonants (five of which have a different form when used at the end of a word). All the letters are capitals. It reads from right to left.

Imagine if English worked the same way. You might come across the phrase:

PHC GB

Without vowels being supplied, you'd be left scratching your head. What words did the writer mean for us to read:

BIG CHAP? BUG CHOP? BOG CHIP?

For centuries, there was only one way to be sure you were correctly reading, pronouncing, and repeating the vowel-less words of a passage in Hebrew: you had to have attended some kind of class or religious gathering during which you heard a trained scribe read the passage orally. *If* you paid careful attention, and *if* you committed what you heard to memory, *then* you would be able later to read that section of Scripture accurately.

Thankfully, the Masoretes created a system to ensure that people would read the words of the biblical text in accordance with proper, longstanding Jewish tradition. By inserting dots and dashes above or below each word's consonants, they indicated for the reader the precise vowel sounds he needed to supply. They also added cantillation (akin to English accent marks) to function as punctuation.

The Masoretes went even further. They filled the margins of their manuscripts with all sorts of detailed notes. They would, for example, note how many words or letters were in a book. Or they would mention how many times a certain word was found in the Hebrew Bible with a certain spelling. With eagle eyes and immense attention to detail, the Masoretes created a finished, standardized text. It is called, fittingly, the Masoretic Text. Some of the manuscripts they produced served as the basis for the printed Hebrew Bibles in use today.

By 930 CE, this authoritative version was completed. The final text (comprised of twenty-four books) is the definitive Tanakh (Hebrew Bible). Orthodox Jews regard this corrected text to be as close as possible a copy of the original biblical text. The Aleppo Codex (see chapter 8) is our best and earliest example of the Masoretic Text. Unfortunately, most of the Torah section has disappeared from the manuscript, either as a result of a fire in Aleppo or theft. Luckily, scholars had examined and recorded much of the textual information preserved in this manuscript before these pages disappeared. Incredibly, the invaluable notebook of one of these scholars lay hidden in an attic until his family discovered it many years later.

Which brings us back to the Ashkar-Gilson Manuscript. It is extremely valuable because it gives us a peek at the consonantal text as it was transmitted generation after generation, and as it was when the Masoretes began their careful finishing of vowel letters and signs and cantillation marks.

In 2007, the study of this manuscript took a great leap forward. The manuscript was put on exhibit at the Shrine of the Book in the Israel Museum, where the most complete Dead Sea Scrolls are housed. Mordechay Mishor of the Academy of the Hebrew Language in Jerusalem noticed the similarity between the Ashkar-Gilson Manuscript and a manuscript that had been held by Jews' College in London. He enlisted the help of Edna Engel of the Hebrew Paleography Project of the Israel Academy of Sciences and Humanities, and she proved that these were part of the same manuscript. With the permission of the owners of both manuscripts, a full scholarly study of these texts was undertaken and published.

Though it lacks vowels and cantillation marks and Masoretic notes—all of which came later—the Ashkar-Gilson Manuscript shows the text of Exodus 15 ("the Song of the Sea") laid out in a kind of brickwork pattern. This symmetrical, stichometric arrangement for poetry (which doesn't appear in the one older text of Exodus 15 preserved at Qumran, although this text does have some extra spacing) helps readers and worshipers know when to sing and when to breathe.

The layout is not only beautiful to behold, but it is also practical in terms of ensuring that later readers will carry on ancient Jewish traditions. It's worth noting that Torah scrolls used in synagogues today have a very similar brickwork layout, some 1,200 to 1,300 years after the Masoretes did their work.

In short, the era following the fall of Jerusalem and continuing into the early Middle Ages was a crucial period in the development of the Hebrew Bible. The rabbis set out to explain the Scripture. The Masoretes embarked on a successful mission to *standardize* it.

What about the Christian Bible during this period?

Between the years 300 and 1000, Christian scholars and scribes were sifting through a variety of Greek texts, much as their Jewish counterparts were evaluating assorted Hebrew manuscripts. If there were a watchword for this era, it would be standardization.

With perseverance and devotion, these learned men puzzled over texts with variant readings and, with fear and trembling, made their best educated guesses about which rendering was better attested. Meanwhile, copyists and monks labored to reproduce these corrected biblical documents accurately. They saw their efforts as a holy calling. Said Cassiodorus, a sixth-century monk, "The scribe preaches with the pen."[2]

Sacred or not, being a scribe was grueling, tedious work. Imagine spending your days in dimly lit and cramped quarters, hunched over documents filled with tiny print. (Eyeglasses, by the way, wouldn't be available until the 1200s.) It's no wonder that one copyist wrote upon finishing a manuscript, "As the harbor is welcome to the sailor, so is the last line to the scribe." (Never mind that he would have to set sail on a new copying project the following day!)

By the late fourth century, Greek language dominance was fading. Latin was replacing Greek as the common language of the Roman Empire. Some in religious academia had even begun to translate the Bible into Latin so that more laypeople could read it.

Translating is a tricky business. The goal, of course, is to take a message expressed in one language and put it into a different language in an accurate and clear way. Yet translators have varying styles. Some adopt a strict and literal word-for-word approach, as in the Richard Rolle Bible. Others embrace a more fluid style—employing common vernacular to express ancient ideas, such as the modern New International Version. Either way, things can, as they say, get lost in translation. It gets even more complicated when one translates from a less-than-accurate translation!

With an obvious demand for a Bible in Latin, and with several versions beginning to pop up, Pope Damasus I (also called Bishop of Rome) saw the need for a standardized Latin translation. He asked one of his advisers, an Italian named Jerome (347–420 CE), to tackle this project.

Jerome was flat-out brilliant. He was passionate about learning and also about helping others learn the Bible. In fact, he once said that ignorance of the Bible was ignorance of Jesus. A former member of an ascetic community who also lived for a while as a hermit in the desert, it's hard to picture Jerome as a prolific writer and classical scholar. But he was.

Jerome agreed to take on the project. He did this translation in a Bethlehem church (the Church of the Nativity), in a small office adjacent to the traditional location of the manger of Jesus's birth. But he was filled with fear and trepidation. He famously said:

> You urge me to revise the old Latin version, and to sit in judgment on the copies of the Scriptures which are now scattered throughout the whole world; and, if they differ from one another, you would have me decide which of them agree with the Greek original. The labor is one of love, but at the same time both perilous and presumptuous. . . . What, then, must I do? The task is beyond me, and yet I dare not decline it. I am a mere unskilled passenger, and I find myself placed in charge of a freighted ship. I have not so much as handled a rowboat on a lake, and now . . . the clouds are black as night, the waves are white with foam.

> For, if our ship drifts into the wished-for haven, I shall be content to be told that the pilotage was poor. But, if through my unpolished language we run aground amid the rough cross-currents of language, you may blame my lack of power, but you will at least recognize my good intentions.[3]

Jerome consulted a *magister Judaeus* (a Jewish teacher) and learned Hebrew as well as other languages so he could study many sources in his work of translating. While other early Christian scribes translated from the Greek Septuagint Bible, Jerome avoided translating from a translation. He rendered the Old Testament into Latin from the original Hebrew. Each time Jerome finished a section of Scripture, he would send his translation to friends for feedback. With each batch, he included an introductory letter. For several centuries, whenever scribes copied Jerome's translation, they included his letters (or "prologues" as they came to be called) in their new manuscripts.

Jerome's Bible became known as the *Vulgate*, which means "common language" in Latin. A perfectionist, Jerome kept revising and refining the work for the rest of his life.

The oldest surviving copy of Jerome's Vulgate is a manuscript known as the Codex Amiatinus. At 2,060 pages, it weighs nearly seventy-five pounds! It was transcribed about 700 CE by scribes in northeast England. Intended as a gift for Pope Gregory, the codex went on a 1,300-mile pilgrimage. After a long stop at the Abbey of San Salvatore, on the slopes of Monte Amiata in southern Tuscany, and a brief stint in Rome, the codex ended up in Florence, Italy, where it survived Allied bombing in World War II and the great flood of 1966.

Scholars agree that Codex Amiatinus has had an interesting history. But it's nothing compared to the codex we'll look at next.

CHAPTER EIGHT

LIGHT IN THE DARKNESS

JEWISH AND CHRISTIAN BIBLES IN THE MIDDLE AGES

There was nothing medieval people liked better, or did better, than sorting out and tidying up.

—C. S. Lewis, The Discarded Image: An Introduction to Medieval and Renaissance Literature

Typically, when people hear the bizarre saga of the Aleppo Codex, they have one of three responses: (1) "How come I've never heard about this before?"(2) "The story *must* be true, if for no other reason than nobody could ever dream up something so outrageous!" (3) "Why hasn't some Hollywood producer made this into a movie? It would surely be a blockbuster."

The story of the Aleppo Codex is the true tale of an ancient book: a beautiful—some would claim "perfect"—Bible completed by the Masoretes in Tiberias in 930 CE. The book then embarked on a wild, 1,000-year journey during which it was stolen, ransomed, relocated, revered, and closely guarded before being smuggled, picked apart, and put in a museum.

Some of the supporting characters in this real-life mystery include a renowned medieval scholar, a tight-knit Jewish community in Syria, an Aleppo cheese merchant, a washing machine, some Israeli secret agents, and a Jerusalem book dealer who died mysteriously.

Sit back and listen to one of the craziest stories you'll hear this year—or any year.

It's called the Aleppo Codex because it spent the bulk of its existence in Aleppo, Syria. However, this unbelievably significant Hebrew Bible was "born" in Tiberias, Israel, in approximately 930 CE. It is the work of the Masoretes (see chapter 7). The famous scribe Solomon ben Buya'a wrote the consonantal text. Aaron ben Asher, the last of the Ben Asher family of Masoretes, is responsible for everything else on the page. This dates its creation to about 1,000 years after the Dead Sea Scrolls.

It's a codex—an early form of a book, with 500 leaves (written on both sides). The leaves are made of *vellum* (calf hides that have been treated, stretched thin, bleached, and cut). At the time of its development and use, such a codex would have been worth a fortune.

Though we have older biblical documents containing portions of Scripture (such as the Dead Sea Scrolls), the Aleppo Codex is the oldest and one of the most revered Hebrew Bibles in existence. It is widely regarded as the most authoritative text in Judaism. Since it was produced by the Masoretes, it features vowel markings or pointings, plus other helps to guide readers in chanting. It also includes many marginal notes.

Around 1040, the codex was purchased by Israel ben Simcha of the Karaite community. (The Karaite movement came into existence in the seventh-century CE and was based on ancient practices that existed long before the spread of the rabbinic tradition.) The Karaite movement established important centers in Israel, Babylonia, Persia, and Egypt, and its scholars were prominent in the study of the Hebrew language, the Tanakh, and Jewish philosophy. The Karaites are distinctive in that they accept only the authority of the written law (the Hebrew Bible) and not the oral law (the Mishnah and Talmud).

When Israel ben Simcha purchased the codex, he moved it to Jerusalem. During its stay in Jerusalem, the codex was routinely brought out on Jewish feast days. Karaite leaders would read from it, after which the book was displayed so that worshipers might marvel at its beauty.

The codex didn't remain in Jerusalem for long. In 1099, Crusaders invaded. Historians tell us they destroyed many things in their path. However, when they stumbled upon this exquisite book, they recognized its value. They seized it (together with some other sacred writings), and they set a steep ransom price for its safe return.

When the wealthy Jews of the Fustat community (the first Muslim capital in Egypt, now part of Old Cairo) heard this news, they were distraught. What would happen if the definitive Hebrew Bible were lost forever? They came up with the ransom price and brought the codex to Cairo, where it remained for almost four centuries.

Ever notice how great people often acquire multiple nicknames? For example, Abraham Lincoln was known as "Honest Abe," "the Great Emancipator" and "the Rail Splitter." Hall of Fame baseball player George Herman Ruth was called "The Babe," "the Bambino," and "the Sultan of Swat."

In Fustat, Egypt, in 1170 there was a great rabbi named Moses ben Maimon. He was a Renaissance man long before the Renaissance ever happened. A noted Torah scholar, he was also renowned as a philosopher and astronomer. And in his free time, he worked as a physician! No wonder people gave him multiple nicknames: "Rambam" (an acronym for Rabbi Moses ben Maimon), "Maimonides" ("ides" means "son of" in Greek), and "the Great

Eagle" (because he soared over the oral law and was able to provide an unparalleled summary).

When Maimonides decided (between 1170 and 1180) to write a definitive, fourteen-volume compilation of Jewish religious law called the *Mishneh Torah*, he used this Masoretic codex as his primary reference for the section "laws of (the writing of) the Torah Scroll." He used this edition because he recognized the Aleppo Codex as the most accurate and authoritative Hebrew manuscript in existence.

In about 1375 the codex was on the move again, this time to Syria. Historians believe that Rabbi Joshua ben David, the great-great-great grandson of Maimonides, personally brought it, along with some other religious manuscripts.

The codex was housed at the Central Synagogue in Aleppo. There it remained under constant, tight security—usually in an iron safe located in a secret crypt called the Cave of Elijah in the rock underneath the building. Only a small, select group had keys. Anyone who wished to see or study the codex had to secure the permission of all those with keys. Even then, scholars were granted only brief access, always under close scrutiny.

Regarded as the greatest of Hebrew Bibles, the Masoretic codex gained multiple nicknames. Some began to call it the "Crown of Aleppo"; others simply referred to it as "the Crown."

To be sure, the entire community treated it like a priceless royal crown. The book was thought to have mystical power. Women who wanted to bear children were convinced that looking at the Crown would enable them to conceive. It was believed that this Tanakh's mere presence secured divine blessing for the community; its absence would result in disaster, perhaps even a plague. All were convinced that if the codex were ever stolen, the thief or thieves would be cursed.

And so this treasure remained in Aleppo for almost 600 years. It survived the Mongol invasion of 1400. It survived the great earthquake of 1822. Then, following 500 relatively peaceful years, came the twentieth century.

In the 1930s, there was a push among Jews to reclaim their heritage. Practically speaking, this meant locating and returning scattered Jewish artifacts to their ancient homeland. Leading up to World War II, scholars like Umberto Cassuto of the Hebrew University of Jerusalem and politicians like Yitzhak Ben-Zvi fretted over the security of the one-of-a-kind Crown of Aleppo.

In 1943, they dispatched one of their colleagues, Yitzhak Shamosh, to try to broker a deal for its return. He was strongly rebuffed by the Jewish elders of Aleppo. However, while in Syria, he met with some younger members of the Aleppo community. They offered to help him formulate and carry out a plot to grab the codex and spirit it to Israel. Because of his conscience (and perhaps also because of the dire curses decreed on anyone who took the book), Shamosh refused.

The concern for the Crown's safety proved to be justified. In late November 1947, the day after the United Nations announced the creation of the state of Israel, a wave of anti-Semitic violence swept across the region. Riots filled the streets of Aleppo, and angry mobs attacked and burned the Central Synagogue. It was initially reported that the Crown of Aleppo had been destroyed. Hearing this news back in Jerusalem, Yitzhak Shamosh was devastated.

But the reports were inaccurate.

No one is really sure exactly how the codex was saved—multiple stories have circulated. But according to journalist Matti Friedman, author of *The Aleppo Codex* (perhaps the most carefully researched account of events), it was Asher Baghdadi, the sexton of Central Synagogue, who returned to the building's smoldering rubble the following morning and retrieved the beloved book.

When new reports began surfacing that perhaps the codex had survived, an antiquities dealer in the United States offered the Syrian government $20 million for the book. In response, the leaders of the Aleppo synagogue, determined to hold on to their revered codex, perpetuated the story of the book's destruction. For the next decade, they hid the Crown at undisclosed locations around Aleppo.

Despite the official story that the codex was lost, whispers of the Crown's survival persisted. Jewish leaders in Israel pressed harder for the book's return. The chief rabbi of Israel annulled the curses associated with the book. Ben-Zvi, who by this time was Israel's second president, appealed to Jewish immigrants from Aleppo living in New York City to use their influence: Would they threaten to withhold financial support from the beleaguered Jewish community in Syria until the codex was returned to Israel?

In 1957, two rabbis in Aleppo decided to act. According to Friedman, they secured the help of Murad Faham, a Jewish cheese merchant. When one of the keepers of the Crown showed up at Faham's house with the precious codex in a sack, Faham's wife wrapped the package in cheesecloth and stuck it inside a washing machine!

Details are conflicting, but somehow Faham was able to smuggle the codex out of Syria, through Turkey, and ultimately to the Israeli port city of Haifa. There he gave the ancient book to a Jewish immigration department employee. It is unclear why Faham did so, when strong evidence exists that he had promised the Aleppo rabbis he would deliver the codex to Isaac Dayan, the senior rabbi of the Aleppo Jews in Israel. Finally in the hands of the Israeli government, the codex reached the desk of President Ben-Zvi.

There are plenty of unsolved mysteries concerning the codex, none bigger than this: at some point, a large chunk of the codex—40% in all, including almost the entire Torah—went missing. To this day no one knows when these 200 pages were lost—before it left Aleppo or after it arrived in Israel. And no one knows where they all are. Fortunately, a handful of the missing pages—said to be worth millions—are rumored to be in the possession of wealthy collectors. Unfortunately, one antiquities dealer who reportedly was selling such codex leaves on the black market was found dead in his hotel room in the mid-1980s!

Even as you read this book, there are arguments over who really owns this piece of history. And there are claims that private investigators have been hired to chase down leads and locate these missing pieces of Israel's rich spiritual legacy. Stories abound about pages of the codex, or pieces of pages, being in the possession of former members of the Aleppo community. If true, none of these individuals seems eager to reunite the missing pages with the rest of the book—probably due to the document's value and also because of the belief that these scraps of antiquity have a kind of mystical power to bless the one who possesses them.

Here is what we know for sure: after a millennium of travel and intrigue, the bulk of the codex has returned to within about 100 miles from where it was created. Given its tumultuous history, it is in remarkable condition. You can see it with your own eyes in Jerusalem at the Shrine of the Book of the Israel Museum.

These facts don't sit well with many. Said Ezra Kassin, "The Aleppo Codex was never meant to be a dead museum exhibit. It must become, once again, the living heart of a living community—of the community of Aleppo, of course, but in a broader sense of the Jewish people and the world."[1] Scholars however, have observed that if the codex had not been removed from Syria, it probably would have been completely destroyed, denying us all this phenomenal link in the history of the Hebrew Bible.

Referring to the curse that would supposedly fall upon the Aleppo community should Judaism's most storied text ever leave the city, Friedman has noted, "You can dismiss that as superstition, but the codex was taken from the synagogue in 1947 and the community was destroyed. There were Jews in Aleppo for more than two millennia, and today not a single one is left."[2]

On the other hand, one could point out that the ongoing Syrian civil war involving ISIS fighters, Syrian troops, and anti-government rebels has left Aleppo in ruins. Had the Aleppo Codex not been removed in 1947, this amazing treasure—and the Jewish community that watched over it—would surely be no more.

The Aleppo Codex is not a complete text, but it is, nevertheless, the oldest copy of the biblical text with the full Masoretic signs and annotations. Ironically, because the codex was kept hidden in modern times by the Jews of Aleppo, most modern Bible editions and translations follow the more available Leningrad Codex, which, for the most part, is identical with the Aleppo text. Jewish tradition rejects the Aleppo text in specific places where it diverges from the vast majority of manuscripts.

Scholars value the Crown of Aleppo because of the amazing accuracy of its vocalization and Masoretic notations. Furthermore, when other accurate medieval manuscripts are compared to the much-older Dead Sea Scroll fragments of the proto-Masoretic type found at Qumran, there is very little variation in the consonantal text. The Crown is proof of a millennium of exacting standards of textual transmission. It also coincides with volumes of scholarship we have from the Masoretes.

With the Aleppo Codex, the Masoretes gave the medieval world an accurate Bible. In that same era, others would step forward and contribute Bibles that were beautiful and readable.

There is much in the Bible about beauty. First and foremost, God is described as beautiful (Psalm 27:4). If God is the "beautiful crown" of his people (Isaiah 28:5), and if his dwelling place (first the tabernacle, then later the temple) was full of "strength and beauty" (Psalm 96:6), then shouldn't God's Bible be similarly adorned?

Such thinking was the catalyst for a new trend in Bible development in Jewish and Christian manuscripts during medieval times: the inclusion of exquisite artwork, fancy borders, and ornate calligraphy. Such decorative efforts were known as *illumination* (from the Latin word *illuminare*, meaning "to light up"). David Lyle Jeffrey has noted that because medieval synagogue worship services involved Torah readings from unadorned scrolls, these eye-popping illuminated Bibles, "expensively produced, were evidently made for private use in families."[3]

One of the best-known examples of an illuminated Bible from the era is the four-volume *Book of Kells*, which contains the four New Testament Gospels in Latin. Believed to have been created at an Irish monastery in 800 CE, the book is, quite simply, gorgeous. With its vibrant colors, the book does light up, and those fortunate enough to glimpse it at Trinity College in Dublin tend to light up too. It, and other Bibles like it, are true works of art.

A prominent example of an illuminated Hebrew Bible is the Cervera Codex. It was completed in the year 1300 by the Spanish Jewish scribe Samuel ben Abraham ibn Nathan and illustrated by the French Jewish illuminator Joseph Hazarfati and the micrographer Abraham ibn Gaon, who penned the commentaries in tiny letters. This codex was later owned by a family from Cordoba.

In 1379 it was in Galicia, where it inspired the Kennicott Bible, a Spanish Jewish masterpiece. In 1804, it was bought by Portugal's Royal Public Library, bringing the magnificent Bible that had left Iberia centuries earlier back to its original home.

In earlier times, Jerome (see chapter 7) had discouraged the practice of illuminating Scripture as extravagant and indulgent. He famously wrote in a letter to Eustochium, "Parchments are dyed purple, gold is melted into lettering, manuscripts are decked with jewels, while Christ lies at the door naked and dying."[4] Proponents, however, ignored such criticism. They believed this kind of beautiful religious art fostered reverential wonder and spiritual devotion (and spurred Bible sales to wealthy individuals).

In 1330 (some sources say 1320), John Wycliffe was born on an English sheep farm. At age sixteen, this bright young man enrolled at Oxford to study theology and philosophy. His studies, however, were interrupted in 1348 when the bubonic plague ("Black Death") swept through Europe.

The epidemic wiped out at least 40% of the British population, though Wycliffe's life was spared. In 1361, the plague returned, claiming one out of every five residents. Once again, Wycliffe dodged death.

By 1374, Wycliffe had, at long last, completed his doctorate and was serving as rector in the parish of Lutterworth. We might not even know his name today were it not for the fact that, over the final ten years of his life, he became embroiled in a very public and bitter feud with church leaders. In his writings and sermons, he attacked several Catholic beliefs and practices. Before long, a number of like-minded followers joined him in calling for sweeping changes in the church. These followers were labeled *Lollards* (from *lollen*, meaning "to mutter"—a name that eventually became a euphemism for "heretics"). Because of his visibility and high profile, Wycliffe was later termed the "Morning Star of the Reformation."

Wycliffe also incurred the ire of the Catholic Church for championing the idea that the Bible should be made available not just to clergy but also to English laity—to common folks—in their everyday language.

"For this reason," Wycliffe argued, "Saint Jerome labored and translated the Bible from divers tongues into Latin that it might after be translated into other tongues. Thus, Christ and his apostles taught the people in that tongue that was best known to them. Why should men not do so now?"[5] The Catholic Church's answer, in so many words, was that when untrained theological minds are given unfettered access to the Bible, heresies may follow.

Wycliffe responded by insisting that the Bible, not the pope, is the voice of Christ on earth. He picked up a quill and began to translate Jerome's Latin Vulgate into the Middle English that was the vernacular of his day. Starting with the Gospels, he worked from Jerome's Latin text. With the help of a team of scribes, but against the wishes of the church hierarchy, he began an effort to produce multiple handwritten English Bible manuscripts.

Before completing the work, and surely not long before the church would have convicted him of heresy, Wycliffe died. One of the Lollards, John Purvey, continued his work and was imprisoned in 1390. Yet another follower, John Hus (or Huss), took up the cause, advocating the idea of giving people a readable Bible—a Bible in their native tongue. For his efforts, Hus was burned at the stake in 1415. As he died, he quoted from the Psalms and prayed for his killers.

Forty-three years after Wycliffe's death, officials felt the need to dig up his body, burn the remains, and hurl his ashes into a tributary of the River Avon.

In medieval times, various people succeeded in making the Bible more accurate, more beautiful, and more readable. In C. S. Lewis's words, the world's greatest book was "sorted out and tidied up."

But that was nothing compared to what lay ahead.

CHAPTER NINE

MR. GOOSEFLESH'S REVOLUTION

The Printing Press and the Bible

The people who are crazy enough to think they can change the world are the ones who do.

—Apple Computer's 1997 "Think Different" television ad

On the clear, cool morning of August 20, 1969, the campus police at Harvard University in Boston were summoned to Widener Library.

On the ground next to the building lay an unconscious man with a large knapsack. Directly above him, police observed a long rope hanging out of one of the library windows.

The man, later identified as twenty-year-old Vido Aras of Dorchester, was rushed to Cambridge City Hospital, where X-rays revealed several skull fractures.

A peek inside Aras's bulging backpack revealed Harvard's 500-year-old copy of the Gutenberg Bible. Its bindings were only slightly damaged.

The Gutenberg Bible is historically significant because it is the first major book of any kind printed in the West using movable metal type. Copies are extremely valuable because they are extremely rare. Fewer than 200 Gutenberg Bibles were printed between 1452 and 1455. Fewer than fifty are known to exist. Only about ten of these copies are in the United States.

Harvard received its Gutenberg from the family of one of its graduates. Harry Widener was a 1907 Harvard alum and a passionate book lover and collector. In March 1912, Harry wrote a bookseller in New York to tell of an upcoming book-buying trip to England and to say that he would be returning "on April 10th on the maiden voyage of the *Titanic*." Near the conclusion of that letter, Widener informed his friend about his grandfather's recent purchase of a Gutenberg Bible. "Is it not great?" he exclaimed. "I wish it was for me but it is not."

A few weeks later, Harry Widener perished with more than 1,500 others in the icy waters of the North Atlantic. In 1944, the Widener family donated its Gutenberg Bible to Harvard in Harry's memory.

Following a thorough investigation, police were able to piece together exactly what had transpired. At closing time on August 19, Mr. Aras hid inside Widener Library while everyone else exited. Under cover of night, he then made his way to the building's roof. From there he rappelled down a rope to a window in the Widener Room, where the university's Gutenberg Bible was on display. He somehow avoided triggering the library's alarm system as he removed the seventy-pound, two-volume Bible from its display case. *The Harvard Crimson*, the school's newspaper, reported that Aras then climbed back out the window and began his descent to the ground. Some forty feet above the ground, he lost his grip on the rope.

In the months following this botched theft, a judge dismissed the charges against Aras, ruling that he was mentally ill and therefore not legally responsible for his actions. And Harvard instituted new security measures for its rare book collection.

The book in the backpack was a product of the tumultuous fifteenth century.

As the Middle Ages were drawing to a close, Europe was ravaged by the Black Death (bubonic plague), which claimed one-third of the population. There were mass migrations and revolts by peasants. The old feudal system (serfs working for wealthy lords on great estates) was being dismantled, and a new middle class was growing. The powerful Catholic Church was shaken by schisms and challenged by reformers like John Wycliffe. Rising literacy rates and a relatively new invention—eyeglasses—meant more people were able to read works by authors like Dante and Chaucer. Workers marveled at technological innovations like the spinning wheel and the blast furnace. The whole world, it seemed, was changing.

By the start of the fifteenth century, the Renaissance was sweeping across Europe. Literature, art, politics, science, religion—every discipline was undergoing a sea change in thinking. Economic conditions improved. Standards of living were better. People were living longer. Suddenly common people had both the time and the means to do more than just eke out a bare existence. The whole world, it seemed, was coming to life.

The Renaissance spurred an insatiable hunger for learning. Monasteries grew in number. Universities began to open their doors to laypeople and not just to clergy in training. The demand for books skyrocketed. Fortunately, rag paper (far less expensive than papyrus) was readily available. Unfortunately, books were still produced by hand, and only the wealthy could afford them. In 1400, a large, well-made book that took a single scribe several years to finish might sell for as much as $10,000 in modern dollars. Public libraries did not yet exist. Kindles and the Internet were still a few years off.

This world in flux is the world into which Johannes Gutenberg was born. He was christened Johannes Gensfleisch (a surname that means "Gooseflesh") between 1396 and 1400 in Mainz, Germany. Details about his early life are sketchy and difficult to piece together. Some sources surmise that the elder "Gooseflesh" must have been a scribe and that young Johannes was inspired to find a more efficient way to produce books after watching his father's dreary labor. Most historians believe, however, that his father was a prominent merchant with an aristocratic family lineage.

As a boy, Johannes was good with his hands. He had a knack for tinkering with mechanical things. He acquired skills as a blacksmith and a goldsmith. In 1411, a backlash against well-to-do families in Mainz forced the Gensfleisch family to flee. Records show they owned property in Alta Villa, another city on the Rhine. There is also evidence they lived for a time in Strasbourg and that Johannes may have studied at the University of Erfurt. In 1419, the elder Gensfleisch died, leaving an inheritance to his son. Historians don't agree on exactly when or why Johannes Gensfleisch came to be known as Johannes Gutenberg. (It's probably a good thing he did, though. Somehow, the "Gooseflesh Bible" doesn't sound nearly as distinguished as the "Gutenberg Bible.")

In his mid-to-late thirties, Johannes Gutenberg became engaged to a woman from Strasbourg. When he contracted a serious case of cold feet, he abruptly broke off the relationship. We only know these details because the girl's family sued him for breach of contract. If the two reconciled, if he married someone else, if he ever had children, history cannot tell us.

We do know that both before and after this broken romance, Gutenberg struggled professionally. He never possessed his father's financial acumen. He was not a good businessman. At one point he got involved in a sketchy, money-losing scheme that involved making and selling polished mirrors to religious pilgrims. Apparently the faithful would use these mirrors to try to catch (and keep) the light reflected off holy relics that were displayed in cathedrals and at other sacred sites.

Such endeavors aside, Johannes invested most of his time and limited funds in trying to master the printing process. He rented a workshop. There he built a press. For much of the 1440s he worked long hours every day learning and perfecting the craft. Local scribe guilds who caught wind of his project (and stood to lose their livelihood if his efforts succeeded) began to spread rumors that behind his curtained windows, Gutenberg was engaged in alchemy—the forerunner of modern science, viewed by some at that time as "dark arts."

Gutenberg ignored the whispers. He only worked that much harder.

Printing something today is so easy, even children can do it. You tap away on your computer, then you click press a few keys. Voila! A document magically materializes from the printer. Worst-case scenario, the printer jams and you have to summon your six-year-old to troubleshoot the situation. Or you call Ed from the IT department. He walks in the room, scowls, and fixes the printer.

In such cases, maybe you have to wait for all of fifteen minutes.

Printing in the olden days was trickier. In fact, it was virtually nonexistent—or at least very primitive. As far back as 3500 BCE, intricately carved cylinder seals were being used to roll impressions into wet clay at the ancient site of Uruk in southern Mesopotamia. In Egypt and China, carved stamps (often made from stone) were being pressed into wax or clay.

By 200 CE, woodcuts were surfacing in Asia. A woodcut is produced when an artist intricately gouges and carves a piece of wood until only the desired artwork is left on the surface. The wood is then inked and pressed on paper, leaving an image.

Centuries later, bookmakers began utilizing this same process, substituting text for pictures. A page of text would be carved (backward) into a big wooden block the size of a printed page. When inked, the block could be pressed onto paper, effectively printing an entire page at once. For each succeeding page, a whole new block of text had to be hand-carved. You can imagine how tedious the process was. Carving page after page of wooden letter blocks was as time-consuming as a scribe copying hundreds of lines of text.

By the eleventh century, a system involving movable type made out of clay had been developed in China. It was never widely used—perhaps because the Chinese language has thousands of characters, instead of just twenty-six letters. By the late 1300s, Korean printers were also experimenting with movable metal type. In 1377, one of them published a book of Zen Buddhist teachings called the *Jikii*—some seventy-five years before Gutenberg's Bible.

People have been known to steal things: fancy old Bibles from college libraries, for example, or the good ideas of someone else. Sometimes, however, people don't steal, as much as they have similar epiphanies. You know the idiom, "Great minds think alike."

While Asian printers were busy doing their thing, half a world away in Germany, Johannes Gutenberg was also seeing the potential in movable metal type. His innovation was to cut individual upper- and lower-case letters out of an alloy of lead, tin, and antimony. These letters were then assembled as desired into forms (usually whole pages of text). The carefully arranged letters were locked into place by placing them into frames designed to fit in the bed of the printing press.

Once Gutenberg locked these molds into wood forms, he could get out his "new and improved" ink (oil-based instead of water-based) and get busy printing. After publishing the desired number of pages, he would break down his forms and reassemble the letters into the next page of text. In other words, Gutenberg's letters were movable and reusable. In Gutenberg's print shop, wood-carvers need not apply.

Still, the learning curve was long and the process slow. Gutenberg's bills were mounting. He had burned through his personal savings as well as some money borrowed from a relative. All those months of tinkering and all those experiments, and Gutenberg had nothing to show for his efforts—except a growing sense that he was on the verge of a breakthrough.

In 1450, he sought out a financier, Johann Fust, a well-to-do lawyer in Mainz. To secure a loan of 800 guilders, Gutenberg put up his printing press as collateral. Flush with new cash, he went to work. He printed small pamphlets and leaflets, getting better, gaining skill, while continuing to dream of printing an entire book. And not just any book but an entire Bible—a Latin Vulgate.

Gutenberg's Bible would be beautiful, two columns per page with forty-two lines in each. He wanted to print 200 copies—at least thirty of those on expensive vellum. But purchasing the 100,000 sheets of paper and 8,000 vellum leaves necessary to complete the project would require yet another infusion of capital.

Gutenberg made another appointment with Fust. Some historians speculate that the shrewd Fust saw two realities: one, that mechanical printing was, indeed, about to become a lucrative new industry; and, two, that Gutenberg was overextended and would never be able to pay his mounting debts. Whether that's true, no one can say. What is clear is that Fust agreed to lend Gutenberg an additional 800 guilders in exchange for a sizable equity share in Gutenberg's printing business. Gutenberg agreed.

The men worked together printing Bibles, with Gutenberg showing Fust the ropes of the printing business. Between 1452 and 1455, they—with several other employees—produced between 180 and 190 Bibles. Wealthy buyers eagerly snatched them up at 30 florins each (about what a clerk would have earned in three years)!

They were gorgeous. In fact, upon seeing a Gutenberg Bible in March 1455, Enea Silvio Piccolomini, the man who would eventually become Pope Pius II, wrote a letter to Cardinal Juan Carvajal and gushed, "The script was very neat and legible, not at all difficult to follow—your grace would be able to read it without effort, and indeed without glasses."[1]

The upside of mechanical printing, in theory at least, is that it can minimize—or eliminate altogether—the human errors that are inevitable when a text is hand-copied multiple times. However, producing an error-free printed Bible requires putting an error-free mold of type on one's printing press.

Looking at it another way, a single scribe making a single mistake produces a single flawed copy of the Bible. Later scribes would redline those mistakes, comparing them against earlier copies. And even today, scholars can identify copying mistakes due to other extant manuscripts of the same story or document. A single *printer*, however, who makes a single mistake produces hundreds, or even thousands, of flawed Bibles! Some of history's most infamous examples include:

- *The Wicked Bible* of 1631. Readers were scandalized to read in Exodus 20:13 these words, "Thou shalt commit adultery." (Rather than, "Thou shalt *not* commit adultery.")
- *The Unrighteous Bible* of 1653 renders 1 Corinthians 6:9, "Know ye not that the unrighteous shall inherit the kingdom

of God." (Rather than, " . . . shall *not* inherit the kingdom of God.")

- *The Fool's Bible* of 1763. This Bible accidentally substitutes "a" for "no" in Psalm 14:1, so that the final printed text reads, "The fool hath said in his heart, there is a God."

A Bible from 1612 (perhaps foreshadowing the dangers inherent in publishing the Scriptures) has the psalmist exclaiming in Psalm 119:161, "Printers [instead of "princes"] have persecuted me without a cause."

Clearly, it pays to have a sharp-eyed editor on staff. A competent proofreader is worthy of his or her wages. Today's better publishers hire skilled copy editors to review the final copy. They proof every word, fact, and punctuation mark.

Let's be clear: Gutenberg didn't "invent" publishing. He wasn't the first to print books with movable type. He wasn't the inventor of paper or the creator of ink (although he did devise a better oil-based ink, less inclined to smear). Gutenberg was a tweaker, a tinkerer, an adaptor. He took existing technologies, improved them, and pushed them in new directions. Primarily because of his vision, ingenuity, and hard work, books became the world's first mass-produced product.

Gutenberg's simple press, engineered with mechanical genius and featuring movable metal type, triggered the Printing

Revolution. Within five decades, hundreds of similar presses across Europe were churning out millions of books. Some of the most influential printing houses were Jewish.

After centuries of royal favor and social success, the Jews in Spain suddenly found themselves in grave danger at the end of the fifteenth century. On March 31, 1492, with the Alhambra Decree, King Ferdinand and Queen Isabella stripped Jews across the Iberian peninsula of their prestigious academic and government positions (serving as diplomats, court advisers, or royal treasury officials) and gave them four months to leave the kingdom. This decree prohibited them from taking any of their valuables.

To make matters worse, this Edict of Expulsion fell on the Ninth of Av, the most tragic day of the Jewish calendar. This was the day in history on which Solomon's Temple had been destroyed by the Babylonians in 586 BCE—and also the day in 70 CE on which the Romans had decimated Herod's Temple!

Students of history may remember 1492 for another famous Spanish milestone. This was the year that Isabella and Ferdinand commissioned Christopher Columbus to sail in search of the New World. Ironically, about the same time that numerous ships were leaving the port of Cadiz, carrying Spanish Jews into exile, the famous explorer Columbus was departing from the Spanish port of Palos.

Though this government-ordered deportation (and the Spanish Inquisition that commenced prior to it) pales next to the twentieth-century Holocaust, it remains as one of the darkest episodes in Jewish history. And yet, as so often happens—good things came from evil events.

This despicable persecution of Spanish Jews resulted in the geographical spread of the printing press. The result was that 1492 ended up being a banner year for Bible publishing. A number of the Jews forced to leave Spain were accomplished publishers. Some of these relocated to Italy, establishing thriving printing businesses in Venice. Others settled in Soncino (where another prominent Hebrew press had been operating—and producing high-quality books—since 1483; in 1488, it had released the first complete edition of the Hebrew Bible). Still other Jewish printers set up shop in Constantinople, Turkey, and Thessaloniki (Salonika), Greece.

In 1517, a Christian publisher in Venice by the name of Daniel Bomberg teamed up with a Jewish scholar known as Felix of Prato to produce *Mikraot Gedolot*, a rabbinic Bible. Bomberg argued for the Jews' rights before the Doge (chief magistrate) of Venice. He fervently supported the rights of Jews and opposed anti-Jewish legislation. But because his partner Felix had converted to Catholicism—and also because the pope had endorsed his work—the Jewish public viewed Bomberg's Bible with skepticism.

As a result, Bomberg released a second version, featuring the Masoretic Text, Aramaic translation (Targum), and medieval Jewish commentaries. For good measure, he had the Jewish scholar Jakob ben Hayim edit it. This 1525 edition became the standard rabbinic Bible among Jews for three and a half centuries! And in the early 1600s, when the King James Bible was being produced, translators relied heavily on Bomberg's rabbinic Bible.

Though he was not Jewish, Bomberg is often called the father of Hebrew typography. Besides being the first to print the Masoretic Text of the Hebrew Bible, Bomberg, working with Jewish scholars, published the first complete Talmud around 1520. His work was of such exquisite quality that it became the benchmark for later printing projects.

Whatever happened to Gutenberg? We can't finish this chapter without concluding his story.

Sadly, in 1455, his Bible dreams came crashing to earth—not unlike Vido Aras and his knapsack did at the Harvard Library in 1969. Unable to repay the large sums he had borrowed from his wealthy business partner, Gutenberg was taken to court by Fust. Gutenberg could only watch as a magistrate awarded his entire printing operation (including his press) to Fust. Gutenberg died thirteen years later, living on a meager pension. He never made a single guilder in profit from his Bible-printing venture.

Though Gutenberg didn't make a fortune by printing Bibles, he made something much more significant: a worldwide difference. His foresight and hard work launched a revolution of printed books that is still changing the world.

By Thomas Edison's classic definition—"Genius is one percent inspiration and ninety-nine percent perspiration"—Gutenberg was a true genius. In 2013, *The Atlantic* asked an esteemed group of engineers, scientists, and entrepreneurs to list the fifty greatest technological breakthroughs since the invention of the wheel. Topping their list was the printing press.

Who knew? A hardworking Bible maker is the father (or at least the grandfather) of the Information Age. Humanly speaking, he is the reason you are holding this book in your hands.

Although if it hadn't been for the folks we'll look at next, you might be reading this book in Latin.

CHAPTER TEN

PLOW BOYS, WOMEN, AND GIRLS

Making the Bible Accessible

I would that [the Scriptures] were translated into all languages so that they could be read and understood not only by Scots and Irish but also by Turks and Saracens. . . . Would that, as a result, the farmer sing some portion of them at the plow, the weaver hum some parts of them to the movement of his shuttle, the traveler lighten the weariness of the journey with stories of this kind!

—Desiderius Erasmus, in "The Paraclesis," the preface to his 1516 Greek and Latin edition of the New Testament

When a *New York Times* reporter asked mountain climber George Mallory in 1923 why he so desperately wanted to scale Mount Everest, he replied famously, "Because it's there."

So far as we know, no journalist ever asked William Tyndale why he was dead set on translating the Bible into English. But if one had, Tyndale's answer surely would have been, "Because that's the only language my countrymen understand."

William Tyndale is only one of the towering figures who lived when the Renaissance and Reformation movements were turning Western civilization on its head (roughly 1475–1550). The list of Tyndale's contemporaries reads like a "who's who" of Western civilization's greatest shapers and shakers of culture: Leonardo da Vinci, Michelangelo, Copernicus, Nostradamus, Machiavelli, Ponce de Leon, Christopher Columbus, Henry VIII, John Knox, John Calvin, and Martin Luther, to name just a few.

What a time to be alive!

And let's not forget Desiderius Erasmus. Born in 1466, about a decade after the Gutenberg Bibles were printed, Erasmus was a key figure in the development of the world's greatest book.

He was the illegitimate son of a Dutch priest. When he was young, he lost both his parents in an outbreak of the plague. Erasmus ended up at a school run by the Brethren of the Common Life (an educational group run by laymen who lived ascetic lives in common). He often chafed against the rigid structure of this

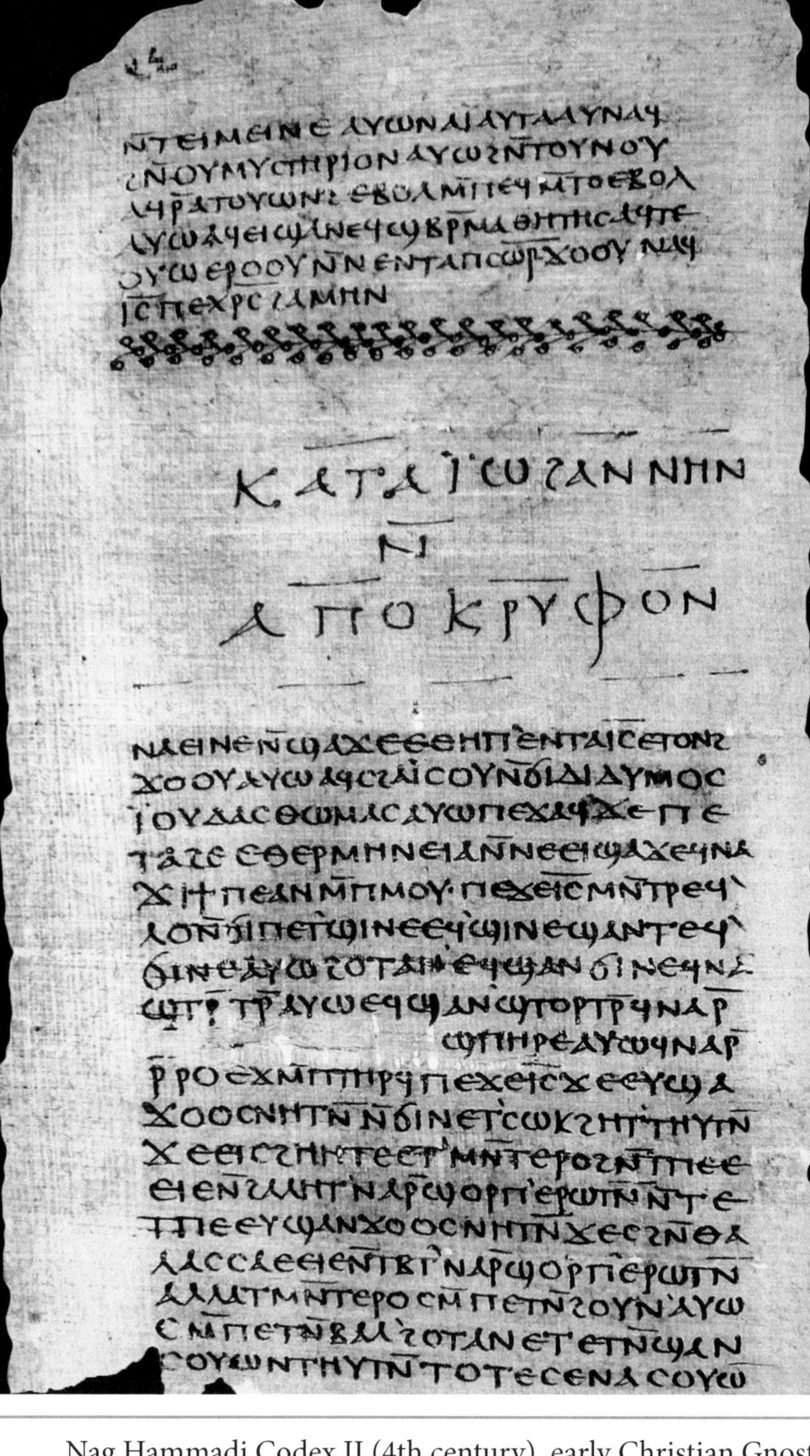

Nag Hammadi Codex II (4th century), early Christian Gnostic texts, including the only complete manuscript of the Gospel of Thomas from antiquity. Written on leather-bound papyrus.

Aleppo Codex (10th century CE), is a Masoretic text containing 500 leaves (double-sided) of the Hebrew Bible.

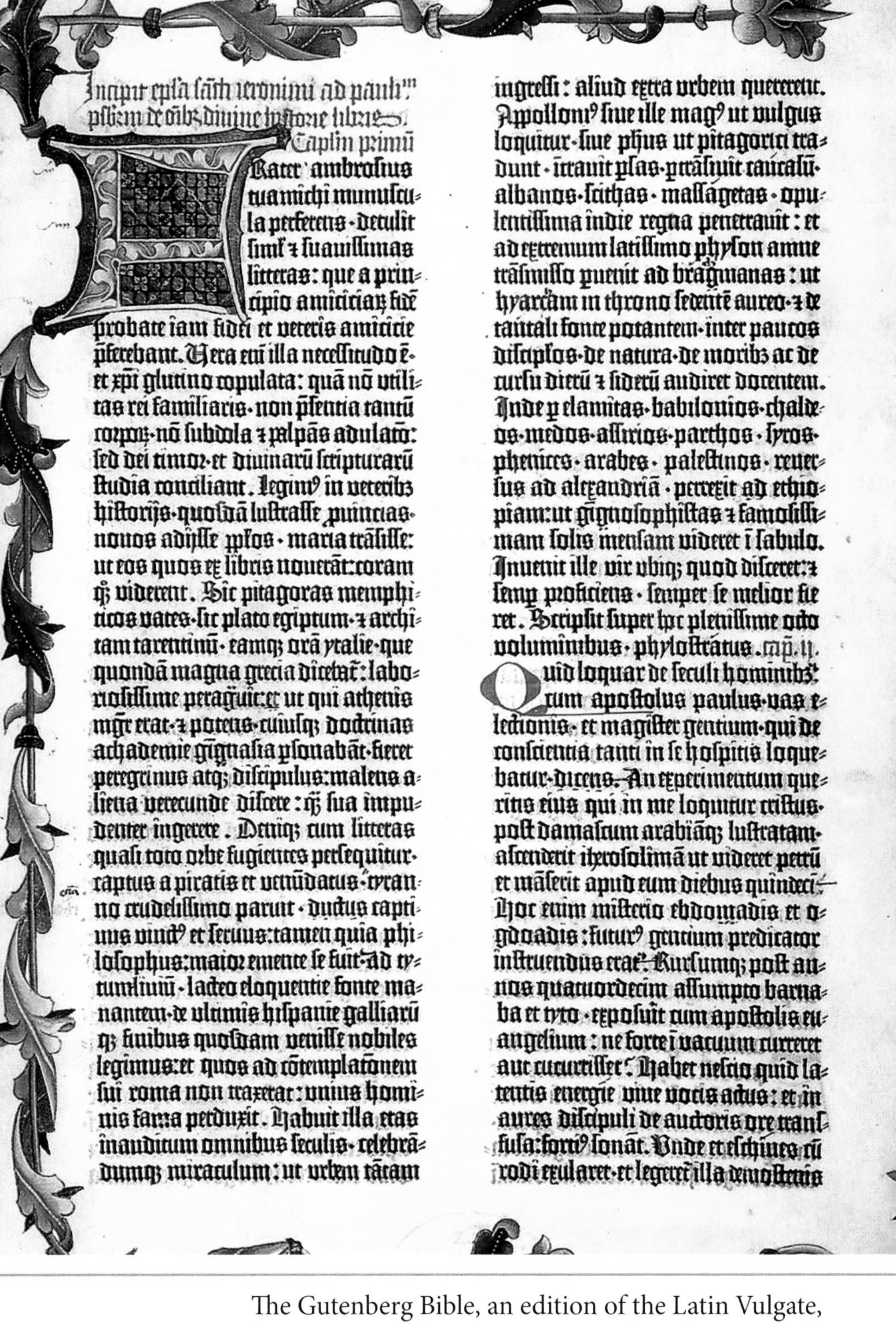

Incipit epistola sancti ieronimi ad paulinum presbiterum de omnibus diuine historie libris.
Capitulum primum

Frater ambrosius
tua michi munuscu-
la perferens detulit
simul et suauissimas
litteras: que a prin-
cipio amiciciarum fidē
probate iam fidei et veteris amicicie
p̄ferebant. Vera enī illa necessitudo ē-
et xp̄i glutino copulata: quā nō utili-
tas rei familiaris · non p̄sentia tantū
corporū · nō subdola et palpās adulatio:
sed dei timor et diuinarū scripturarū
studia conciliant. Legimus in veteribus
historiis · quosdā lustrasse prouincias ·
nouos adisse populos · maria trāsisse:
ut eos quos ex libris nouerāt: coram
quoque viderent. Sic pitagoras memphi-
ticos vates · sic plato egiptum · et archi-
tam tarentinū · eamque orā ytalie · que
quondā magna grecia dicebatur: labo-
riosissime peragrauit: et ut qui athenis
magister erat · et potens · cuiusque doctrinas
achademie gignasia p̄sonabāt · fieret
peregrinus atque discipulus: malens a-
liena verecunde discere: quam sua impu-
denter ingerere. Denique cum litteras
quasi toto orbe fugientes persequitur ·
captus a piratis et venūdatus · tyran-
no crudelissimo paruit · ductus capti-
uus vinctus et seruus: tamen quia philosophus: maior emente se fuit · Ad ty-
tumliuiū · lacteo eloquentie fonte ma-
nantem · de ultimis hispanie galliarū
que finibus quosdam venisse nobiles
legimus: et quos ad cōtemplationem
sui roma non traxerat: unius homi-
nis fama perduxit. Habuit illa etas
inauditum omnibus seculis · celebrā-
dumque miraculum: ut urbem tantam

ingressi: aliud extra urbem quererent.
Apollonius siue ille magus ut vulgus
loquitur · siue philosophus ut pitagorici tra-
dunt · intrauit p̄sas · p̄transiuit caucasū ·
albanos · scithas · massagetas · opu-
lentissima indie regna penetrauit: et
ad extremum latissimo phison amne
trāsmisso peruenit ad bragmanas: ut
hyarcam in throno sedentē aureo · et de
tantali fonte potantem · inter paucos
discipulos · de natura · de moribus ac de
cursu dierū et siderū audiret docentem.
Inde per elamitas · babilonios · chalde-
os · medos · assirios · parthos · syros ·
phenices · arabes · palestinos · reuer-
sus ad alexandriā · perrexit ad ethio-
piam: ut gignosophistas et famosissi-
mam solis mensam videret in sabulo.
Inuenit ille vir ubique quod disceret: et
semper proficiens · semper se melior fieret. Scripsit super hoc plenissime octo
voluminibus · phylostratus. Capitulum ii.
Quid loquar de seculi hominibus:
cum apostolus paulus vas e-
lectionis · et magister gentium · qui de
consciencia tanti in se hospitis loque-
batur · dicens. An experimentum que-
ritis eius qui in me loquitur cristus.
post damascum arabiāque lustratam ·
ascenderit ierosolimā ut videret petrū
et mānserit apud eum diebus quindecim.
Hoc enim misterio ebdomadis et o-
gdoadis: futurus gentium predicator
instruendus erat. Rursumque post an-
nos quatuordecim assumpto barna-
ba et tyto · exposuit cum apostolis eu-
angelium: ne forte in vacuum curreret
aut cucurrisset. Habet nescio quid la-
tentis energie viue vocis actus: et in
aures discipuli de auctoris ore trans-
fusa: fortius sonat. Unde et eschines cū
rodi exularet · et legeretur illa demostenis

The Gutenberg Bible, an edition of the Latin Vulgate,
printed in 1455–1456 by Johannes Gutenberg (1400–1468).

Solomon Schechter (1847–1915), rabbi, scholar, and educator, founder and president of the United Synagogue of America, and president of the Jewish Theological Seminary of America. He discovered the Cairo Genizah in 1896.

The *Book of Kells* (ca. 800 CE) is an illuminated manuscript of the Gospels written in Latin by monastics from England, Scotland, and Ireland.

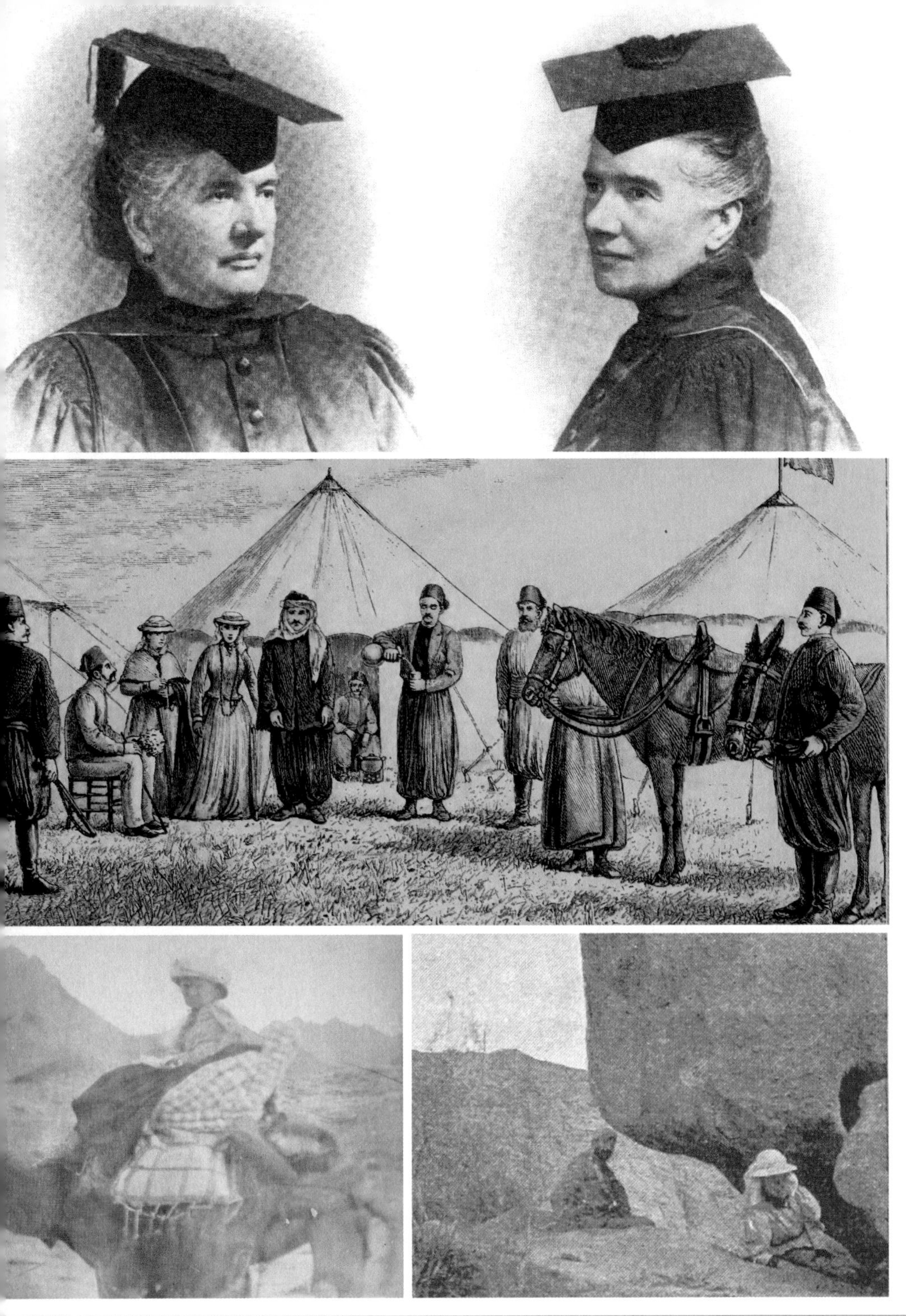

Agnes Smith Lewis (1843–1926) and Margaret Smith Gibson (1843–1920) were Semitic language scholars. These twins discovered the Syriac Sinaiticus and worked with the Codex Climaci Rescriptus.

Leaves from the Codex Climaci Rescriptus which were catalogued by Agnes Smith Lewis and Margaret Smith Gibson. These folios are part of the Museum of the Bible collection.

cheerless bunch, yet he discovered a love for reading and learning. Energized by his classical studies, he decided to become an Augustinian monk.

In 1492—while Columbus was sailing the ocean blue and Spanish Jews were being exiled—Erasmus was being ordained into the Catholic priesthood. He went to Paris to pursue further theological studies. He traveled widely, enjoying every opportunity to dialogue with great theological minds.

While in England in 1499, he met John Colet, the scholar who would eventually become dean of St. Paul's Cathedral in London. Colet's teaching inspired Erasmus to learn Greek, the language of the New Testament. He mastered it quickly.

Erasmus was a prolific and popular writer. Many considered him the leading scholar of his time (a staggering compliment when you consider his brilliant contemporaries). In his famous essay *In Praise of Folly*, Erasmus skewered the Catholic Church for what he considered to be certain excesses. He mocked miracle stories in which healings were attributed to the power of relics. He railed against the purchase of indulgences (official papers signifying forgiveness of sins that were used in ways he found offensive—a view shared by many modern Catholic writers).

In 1516, Erasmus unveiled a combined Latin and Greek edition of the New Testament known as *Novum Instrumentum omne*. This was the first time the Greek New Testament had ever been published via the printing press. Passages appeared in both languages, side-by-side, to allow for comparison. This landmark work gave scholars direct access to the New Testament's original

Greek instead of the church's Latin. It sparked new interest in translating the Bible from its original languages. Erasmus's New Testament would soon become a driving force in Martin Luther's work and the Protestant Reformation. Erasmus's edition created a defining moment in the history of biblical transmission.

This New Testament prepared by Erasmus is known as the *Textus Receptus* (the "Received Text") and for centuries afterward was regarded as the most reliable and authoritative Greek text. (Some conservative Christians still believe this to be the case.) It served as the basis for William Tyndale's New Testament (1526) and, later, the King James/Authorized Version (1611; see chapter 11), as well as the New King James Version (1982).

Erasmus's hope was that his scholarly labors might lead to better, more lay-friendly versions of the Bible. He explained:

> I disagree very much with those who are unwilling to allow that Holy Scripture, translated into the vulgar tongue, be read by the uneducated, as if Christ taught such intricate doctrines that they could scarcely be understood by very few theologians, or as if the strength of the Christian religion consisted in men's ignorance of it. The mysteries of kings, perhaps, are better concealed, but Christ wishes His mysteries published as openly as possible. . . .
>
> Let all the conversations of every Christian be drawn from this source. . . . Only a very few can be learned, but all can be Christian, all can be devout, and—I shall boldly add—all can be theologians.[1]

Though Erasmus and Martin Luther never met, the older man's writings deeply affected the younger Luther. Later, when Erasmus found himself agreeing with many of Luther's anti-Catholic writings, Erasmus became conflicted. As a Catholic priest, Erasmus tried to stake out a neutral position in the growing theological conflict between Luther and the Catholic Church. However, Erasmus ended up a bit like the poor Civil War soldier who wore a gray coat and blue pants into battle—and got fired at by both sides! He later lamented, "Some claim that since I do not attack Luther I agree with him, while the Lutherans declare that I am a coward who has forsaken the gospel."[2]

Though Erasmus died suddenly in 1536 from a violent attack of dysentery, he did live long enough to see some of his wishes come true. Martin Luther used his Greek New Testament to give German farmers and weavers a Bible they could hum and sing in their native German while they worked.

The son of a copper miner, Martin Luther (1483–1546) attended Latin school as a boy. At age thirteen, he enrolled at the University of Erfurt to study law. When he was twenty-two, he got caught one evening in a violent thunderstorm. When he was nearly struck by lightning, he cried out in terror to St. Anne (the patron saint of miners). In that desperate prayer, Luther promised to become a monk if God would spare his life. When God did, Luther kept his word.

The ex-law student threw himself fully into monastic life. Outwardly, Luther was the picture of pure devotion. Inwardly, however, he was tormented by a powerful sense of being far from God. His solution was to try harder. He earned a doctorate in Bible and began teaching at Wittenberg. It was during this time, while meditating on Romans 1:17, that Luther came to understand the New Testament teaching of salvation by faith alone, not by human effort or via the sacraments of the church. This came, in part, through his study of the text in Greek. For Luther, this was not a fleeting moment of intellectual insight; it was a lightning bolt to his very soul. He later wrote of this experience, "I felt as if I were entirely born again and had entered paradise itself through the gates that had been flung open."[3]

Luther developed a consuming passion for Scripture, saying, "The Bible is alive, it speaks to me; it has feet, it runs after me; it has hands, it lays hold of me."[4] Not only did he want to know the Scriptures, but he also wanted to help others understand them. He studied constantly. The more he studied, the more he began to question certain beliefs and practices of the church.

Diplomacy and tact, however, were never Luther's strong suits. He served up frequent criticisms, with an occasional side order of crassness. We can't repeat here many of the names he hurled at the Catholic hierarchy (and sometimes at his fellow reformers).

In 1517 (the year after Erasmus published his Greek New Testament), Luther nailed his famous Ninety-Five Theses to the cathedral door at Wittenberg. This was Luther's grocery list of grievances of what he perceived as the Catholic Church's doctrinal flaws.

For the next four years, Luther and the Catholic Church engaged in a heated theological war. In 1519, Luther claimed publicly that a simple layman armed with the Scriptures was preferable to the pope and one of his councils *without* the Bible.

Luther learned that when you speak truth to power, you'd best get ready for power to respond. Pope Leo X labeled Luther a wild boar in the Lord's vineyard and accused him of heresy. He stood trial and was excommunicated.

Thankfully, Luther had friends (or at least one sympathizer) in high places. Frederick III, also known as Frederick the Wise, was an elector in the Holy Roman Church. Electors were prominent churchmen, the next best thing to religious royalty. Almost like a religious, Renaissance version of the modern US Electoral College, the electors were the powerful group that chose new popes.

Frederick had founded the University of Wittenberg (where Luther taught). He was a quirky man who collected thousands of holy relics—supposed hay from Christ's manger, an alleged twig from Moses's burning bush, and so forth. Though he remained a committed Catholic, Frederick quietly agreed with many of Luther's criticisms. Fearing for Luther's safety, Frederick staged a highway "kidnapping." He arranged for his men to grab Luther as he returned from his trial at Worms. The renegade priest spent almost a year in hiding at Frederick's Wartburg Castle, shielded from the pope's edict.

While there (1521–1522), this "wild boar" of a man was unable to sit still. He decided to translate the New Testament into German so that his countrymen could read Christ's truth for themselves.

But instead of working from the Latin Vulgate (the officially sanctioned Bible of the Roman Catholic Church), Luther went directly to the Greek text. He used the recently published second edition of Erasmus's Greek New Testament.

To ensure that his new translation utilized up-to-date German idioms and everyday expressions, Luther (introducing himself as *Junker Georg*, or "Farmer George") often slipped into nearby villages to eavesdrop on the conversations of common people. Some accounts say that Luther finished his great translation project in a mere eleven weeks!

Whether that timetable is true remains a matter of dispute, but this much is verifiable: Luther's translation was wildly popular with the German people (if not the church hierarchy). Linguists agree that Luther's Bible greatly influenced the development of the modern German language.

Why did Luther choose the approach he did? What motivated his labor? Hear his own words:

> We must inquire . . . of the mother in the home, the children on the street, the common man in the marketplace. We must be guided by their language, the way they speak, and do our translating accordingly. That way they will understand it and recognize that we are speaking German to them.[5]

> This I can testify with a good conscience—I gave it my utmost in care and effort, and I never had any ulterior motives. I have neither taken nor sought a single penny for

> it, nor made one from it. Neither have I sought my own honor by it; God, my Lord, knows this. Rather I have done it as a service to the dear Christians and to the honor of One who sitteth above.[6]

In his later years, Luther battled a host of illnesses—vertigo, arthritis, angina, and kidney stones. None of this kept him from a busy schedule. He translated the Old Testament into German (a project he completed in 1534). He preached, wrote voluminously, got cranky, and even wrote a number of outrageous anti-Semitic works—including his highly inflammatory "On the Jews and Their Lies" (1543). Three years later, at age sixty-two, his body finally wore out. Luther had a stroke and died.

He was buried beneath the pulpit in the Castle Church at Wittenberg. Though Luther was credited with launching the Protestant Reformation, his unfortunate attacks on the Jews were utilized by the provocateurs of the Holocaust. The Lutheran denomination, like most of the world, has roundly denounced Luther's anti-Semitism. Simultaneously, like millions of other Protestants, they appreciate his work on key biblical doctrines gleaned from reading texts in their original languages.

A decade after Luther's death, and about two decades after that of Erasmus, Pope Paul IV placed the writings of both Erasmus and Luther—including Luther's German Bible—on the Index of Prohibited Books.

Most kids are addicted to sports, TV, sugary food, or video games. It was said of young William Tyndale (ca. 1494–1536) that, his mind was "singularly addicted" to the Scriptures.[7] At sixteen he enrolled at Magdalen College in Oxford, eventually finishing up his studies at Cambridge.

He emerged from his schooling with a vibrant faith and an all-consuming conviction that it was impossible for anyone to know God apart from his written Word. Upon seeing a copy of Luther's German New Testament, Tyndale saw his own future. He would produce the first English Bible so that English-speaking peoples, even commoners, might come to understand the Christian teaching of salvation by grace and through faith. "I had perceived by experience," he explained, "how that it was impossible to stablish the lay people in any truth, except the scripture were plainly laid before their eyes in their mother tongue, that they may see the process, order, and meaning of the text."[8]

Since Greek was one of the several languages Tyndale already knew, he, like Luther, decided to work primarily from the esteemed Greek text of Erasmus, rather than the Latin Vulgate of Jerome.

In 1523, Tyndale eagerly (and naively) approached Cuthbert Tunstall, the bishop of London, with his plan. He wanted the church's permission and blessing—and ideally, some funding. "Absolutely not!" he was told. The project that he saw as vital and noble, the church viewed as dangerous, even heretical. Their fear was not without precedent, as the dissemination of misunderstood or radical biblical teachings had played out various times in history.

Undaunted, Tyndale packed his books and his bags. He moved to Europe and went to work. Within two years, he had produced and published—with the help of Peter Schoeffer, a printer in the German city of Worms—3,000 copies of the New Testament in modern English.

Historians tell us Tyndale's Bibles were smuggled back into England inside barrels of flour and bolts of cloth. When these English Scriptures began popping up here and there, the nation's civic and religious leaders—King Henry VIII, Cardinal Wolsey, Sir Thomas Moore, and Bishop Tunstall—were united in their fury. They launched a campaign to seize or purchase every available copy of this "testament of Tyndale's master, Antichrist." Anyone in possession of a Tyndale New Testament was punished. All retrieved Bibles were burned.

In one sense, this plan worked. Today, copies of the first edition of the Tyndale New Testament are so rare they are worth thousands of US dollars. In another way, the plan backfired badly. Official purchases of Tyndale's black-market Bible—an organized effort to get the Bible out of circulation—gave him the funding he needed to print even more copies of a corrected edition!

With phase one of his mission accomplished, Tyndale moved, for obvious security reasons, to Antwerp. There, he was able to work unopposed for almost a decade. He corrected his New Testament translation and changed certain terms to align more closely with Luther's Protestant teachings. He also added some strong anti-Catholic marginal notes.

Tyndale learned Hebrew so that he could translate the Old Testament into English. Never one to sit still, Tyndale also spent time writing and publishing religious tracts and books. On Saturdays, his day off, he ministered to the poor!

Even in hiding, Tyndale remained, in the eyes of the church, public enemy number one. Besides his desire for an English translation, he also drew Henry VIII's ire for opposing the annulment of his marriage. Henry then requested Emperor Charles V's help, and through contacts in Brussels, Tyndale's safe zone would disappear. When it became clear Tyndale had no intentions of suspending his efforts to flood England with his Bibles and Protestant teachings, someone—it's not clear who—orchestrated and funded a plot to find and arrest him.

A silver-tongued ex-politician named Henry Phillips showed up in Holland and befriended Tyndale. Thomas Poyntz, Tyndale's closest friend and most trusted associate, became suspicious of Phillips's intentions. He shared his concerns, but Tyndale dismissed his objections.

Sure enough, Phillips eventually succeeded in luring England's most wanted man away from his home. Tyndale was apprehended in one of Antwerp's winding alleyways and taken to the castle of Vilvoorde (which served at that time as a regional prison). Charged by Catholic Church officials with heresy, Tyndale was imprisoned for about a year and a half. There remained serious concern about common people having access to such an important text in their own language.

The historian of the martyrs, John Foxe, claimed that Tyndale made the most of this time. He allegedly converted his jailer to the Protestant Christian faith. In 1535, he wrote a letter (in Latin) that sheds light on his incarceration. The letter echoes the final new Testament epistle (2 Timothy 4:13). Tyndale asked for warmer clothing (specifically a hat, a coat, some cloth to patch his leggings). He also requested a lamp to push back the loneliness and darkness of his long nights. Finally, he pleaded for a Hebrew Bible, grammar, and dictionary so that he might continue his translation work.

Tyndale's trial, such as it was, ended up being a back-and-forth paper debate that took months. While he waited, he completed his translation of the Pentateuch, and all together, about half of the Old Testament.

The very Bible that Tyndale would die for, and that he had translated into English, was filled with statements that must have come to mind during his final days, such as, "Hope deferred makes the heart sick, but a desire fulfilled is a tree of life" (Proverbs 13:12).

In 1536, Bible translator William Tyndale was condemned as a heretic. First, church officials forced him to participate in a "degradation ceremony" (a ritual removal from the priesthood). Tyndale's hands were scraped symbolically. Bread and wine (representative of the Eucharist) were given to him, then taken from him. His priestly vestments were removed dramatically, one by one.

Later, the forty-something-year-old Tyndale was marched by secular authorities into a public square. There he was made to stand atop a pile of logs and kindling that had been dusted with gunpowder. Guards lashed him to an upright post. They placed a rope and chain noose around his neck. Given an opportunity to say some final words, Tyndale prayed simply, "Lord, open the king of England's eyes."[9] Following that, he was strangled to death and his body burned.

Some would label Tyndale's life "tragic." Yet he is hailed by most scholars today as the father of the English Bible. Perhaps as significant as his translation work was his dying prayer—which turned out to be amazingly prescient.

CHAPTER ELEVEN

ONE BILLION COPIES AND COUNTING

The Story of the King James Bible

Why all the fuss about an old translation of an ancient book? There are two reasons: first, it is the founding text of the British Empire (including breakaway colonies such as the United States), and was carried to every corner of the English-speaking world by migrants and missionaries; second, it matters now, both as a religious text and as the finest embodiment of English prose.

—Gordon Campbell, professor of Renaissance Studies, University of Leicester

When NASA astronauts Alan Shepard and Edgar Mitchell stepped onto the moon's surface on February 5, 1971, it was one small step for golf and one giant leap for God's Word.

The cool and cocky Shepard pulled out a makeshift six-iron he had smuggled aboard *Apollo 14* and promptly whacked a couple of golf balls across the lunar surface. The spiritually minded Mitchell, meanwhile, secretly carried in his spacesuit one hundred copies of the King James Bible.

We know what you're thinking: *That must have been one extra-large spacesuit.*

But it wasn't. The Bibles were on microfilm—each one only an inch (or an inch and a half) square. Yet each one contained all 1,245 pages of the King James Bible!

The tiny Bibles were the brainchild of the Apollo Prayer League, a group that formed following the fire aboard *Apollo 1* that claimed the lives of astronauts Ed White, Gus Grissom, and Roger Chaffee. The founder of the group, John Stout, a NASA engineer, had been especially close to White.

Apollo 14 wasn't the microfilm Bibles' first excursion to the moon. They had also been aboard *Apollo 12*—though nobody remembered to move them into the lunar module (meaning, they never touched down on the moon but only orbited it in the command module). These tiny Scriptures had flown again on *Apollo 13*. But with all that mission's mechanical in-flight troubles (popularized by the Tom Hanks movie of the same name), the Bibles not only didn't make it to the moon's surface, but they almost didn't make it back to earth!

The third time proved to be the proverbial charm. Mitchell, mostly to honor his late friend Ed White, stuck the microfilm Bibles in a zippered pocket before he went for one of his two lunar strolls. Upon his return to earth, Upon his return to earth, Mitchell, who had kept a few of the mini Bibles, gave them to John Stout, the founder of the Apollo Prayer League.

Few people knew about these Lunar Bibles until recent years. That's probably because NASA listed them on Apollo flight manifests as "microfilm packets" rather than "microfilm Bibles." Then, in 2010, the elderly, destitute Stout—and his wife—became wards of the state of Texas. When one of the Lunar Bibles sold at Sotheby's for $56,000 in 2012, and when others also began coming up for auction, Texas started filing restraining orders and claiming custody rights.

Suddenly the microfilm King James Bibles were big news.

The story of how the King James Bible went to the moon is interesting. But the story of how it came to us might be even more fascinating.

Do you remember that William Tyndale was condemned to death in 1536 for the "crime" of translating the Bible into the English language? And do you remember what he prayed moments before his execution? "Lord," he whispered, his neck in a noose, "open the king of England's eyes."

Just three years later, Henry VIII, king of England, saw the light! He *demanded* a Bible in the common vernacular. First, he gave his royal authorization to Miles Coverdale (Tyndale's former assistant and proofreader) to prepare such a Bible. Then he decreed that each church in England would be required to purchase a copy and put the Bible in a convenient place where all parishioners could see and read it.

Coverdale got busy. He essentially took Tyndale's unfinished Bible and reworked it. Using Jerome's Latin Vulgate, he translated the remaining Old Testament books and the Apocrypha. Then he either took out or toned down Tyndale's inflammatory anti-Catholic notes.

The result was the Great Bible, a name that had less to do with the work's quality and more to do with its size. The finished product was massive. Because many churches chained the Bible in place to ward off thieves, it was also sometimes called the Chained Bible. In 1540, when a second edition was released with a new preface by Thomas Cranmer, some began referring to it as Cranmer's Bible.

What prompted Henry's sudden about-face? Why his sudden desire for an English Bible? To answer that question, we need a bit of historical context.

In the early Middle Ages, Christianity had two centers of administrative power, most notably in Rome and Constantinople—the Western Church and the Eastern Church. Rome would eventually declare itself the official headquarters of the Christian religion and the pope the worldwide leader. Instead of the hodge-podge of denominations that we see today, the Christian Church was united—at least among the majority of Christians who recognized the pope in Rome. It was *catholic* (meaning "universal") in nature.

During this time, the Eastern Church (the Orthodox Church) had developed in many of areas where Paul had planted churches. Because many of those areas had been settled by Greeks in centuries earlier, the Eastern Church was commonly associated with Greek heritage. In 1054, the church in Rome (the West) and the church in Constantinople (the East) could no longer ignore their differences, and an East-West Schism occurred. (Therefore, when we speak of either the Roman or the Orthodox Church as catholic, or universal, this history needs to be kept in perspective.)

More change was stirring in in the fourteenth and fifteenth centuries. We have already mentioned dissident priests like John Wycliffe and William Tyndale, and monks like Martin Luther who were speaking out against certain beliefs and long-standing practices of the church.

Then along came an unhappily married king.

King Henry VIII's first wife, Catherine of Aragon, had not given him a male heir (their daughter Mary was the only one of their five children to survive infancy). What's more, Henry had become enamored with the younger Anne Boleyn. In 1527, the king asked Pope Clement VII for an annulment so that he might marry his new love. When the pope did not consent, Henry went ahead with his plans. When the pope excommunicated the king, Henry decided to break completely with the Roman Catholic

Church. In 1534, he declared himself the head of the Church of England and required his subjects to swear allegiance to the same.

This is the reason King Henry VIII was suddenly interested in having an English Bible—he was the leader of the brand-new Church of England! And his primary reasons for starting a new church were marital, not theological. Given all this history, it's not a stretch to say that a messy royal divorce triggered a messy religious divorce. And it's not a stretch to say that, in the end, it was a bad marriage that led to the birth of the English Bible.

It may have been Henry's royal chutzpah that emboldened others to push for even greater religious change. Those who protested certain Catholic ideas (called Protestants) or wanted deeper theological reforms (called Reformers) or a purer, more biblically based church (called Puritans) began to speak up.

When King Henry died in 1547, he left England, quite literally, in a royal mess. His successor was his nine-year-old son Edward VI, who died 1553 at age fifteen.

Enter Mary Tudor, Henry's daughter by his first wife, Catherine of Aragon. A devout Catholic, Mary had one desire: to make England loyal to the pope in Rome once again. Thus began her brief but violent persecution of Protestants, earning her the nickname "Bloody Mary" (even though Protestant leaders also were known to put dissenters to death). Many of those who escaped with their lives did so by fleeing to the European continent. Geneva became a refuge for Reformers like John Knox and Miles Coverdale. It also became, in 1560—two years after Mary's death—the birthplace of the Geneva Bible.

The Geneva Bible was revolutionary in that it was designed for daily use by individual believers, not for display in parish churches. It was more compact than other Bibles. It featured clear language. It was the first English Bible to embrace the verse numbering system devised by Rabbi Isaac Nathan (for the Hebrew Bible, 1448) and Frenchman Robert Etienne (for the New Testament, 1551). The Geneva Bible included explanatory notes from a Puritan perspective and short book introductions. Because it was affordable, the masses loved it. It soon became the preferred Bible of William Shakespeare and John Bunyan. It was also the Bible of choice among the pilgrims who sailed on the *Mayflower*.

The unexpected popularity of the user-friendly Geneva Bible spurred a response by other religious groups. In 1568, the Church of England, with Queen Elizabeth I on the throne, unveiled the Bishops' Bible, so-called because most of the scholars who worked on it were bishops in the church. Essentially a revision of the Great Bible, the Bishops' Bible was a definite upgrade; however, with its formal wording, it was unable to dislodge the Geneva Bible from its place as the favorite holy book of the English people.

Catholics, now a minority group in England, responded with the Douay-Rheims Bible, released in sections between 1582 and 1610. Working from the Latin Vulgate, translators and scholars in the French university towns of Douay and Rheims produced a work full of notes defending the Catholic faith from the critiques of the Reformers. Subsequent revisions—especially one by Richard Challoner—greatly increased the readability of the text.

So, by the beginning of seventeenth century, the Bible market in England was flooded—the Great Bible, the Geneva Bible, the Bishops' Bible, the Douay-Rheims Bible. Some people would have said, "Please! No more! We have enough English Bibles!"

King James I, a much younger cousin of Queen Elizabeth, and England's new thirty-seven-year-old monarch, thought otherwise.

It's doubtful anyone would have described James Stuart as "dashing." Portraits of the new king reveal a wary-looking man with reddish hair and a prominent, pointed nose. The word that comes to mind is *foxlike*. Historians tell us King James I was impatient and clever, strange and idealistic. Said one Frenchman, "He is never still for a moment, but walks perpetually up and down the room . . . he is an old young man."[1]

James began his reign in 1603. The British Empire was filled with religious friction. On one side, James had the official (and powerful) Church of England, with its hierarchical form of government that few people liked. On the other side were the cantankerous Puritans, who regarded the state church as too tolerant of Catholicism. They longed for a "pure" church, one without bishops and freed from every vestige of Catholic pomp and ritual. In fact, before James even assumed the throne, the Puritans had sent him a petition asking for reforms in the church.

Feeling pressured from all sides, and desiring to reign over a peaceful nation, James did what most leaders do when they're not sure what else to do—he called a meeting. He invited a host of religious movers and shakers to Hampton Court Palace.

In January 1604, these leaders brought their religious grievances—and their hidden agendas—to the massive royal estate in the southwest suburbs of London. Only four Puritans were invited. When they were excluded from the opening-day assembly, they sensed they weren't going to be major players at this conference. Later, when James mocked and bullied them for their Puritan beliefs in a private meeting, they were sure of it. Finally, one of the four, John Reynolds, perhaps just trying to change the subject, politely asked, "May your Majesty be pleased that the Bible be new translated?"[2]

James's dislike of the popular Geneva Bible was no secret. Because of its many anti-royalist marginal notes, he labeled it "untrue, seditious, and [full of] dangerous and traitorous conceits."[3] In suggesting a new Bible translation, Reynolds may have been grasping at straws, but his impulse was a stroke of genius. The translation idea intrigued the king. To be fair, he was less interested in biblical scholarship than he was in political stability. But perhaps the former could bring about the latter? Maybe a new Bible would unify his country's religious factions and boost his own popularity with his subjects?

On January 17, King James gave the go-ahead for this project.

Committees are notorious for disorganization and disagreement. How many times have you seen a team of people come together, argue fiercely, reluctantly agree on an ill-conceived plan, then execute it poorly (or not at all)? There are good reasons the eminent British historian Arnold Toynbee once reportedly quipped, "I don't believe a committee can write a book."

King James believed otherwise. He ordered Archbishop Richard Bancroft to begin assembling a translation team.

In all, before the project was completed, fifty-four learned men participated in this task. These scholars were divided into six groups of eight men each. Each team was then given a section of the Bible. (The Tanakh or Old Testament was broken down into three parts, the New Testament into two, and one team was assigned the Apocrypha.) The six committees were assigned to work in three different locations: Westminster, Cambridge, and Oxford.

The king's instructions were fairly simple and straightforward. He wanted the new Bible to mirror the Bishops' Bible as closely as possible. The translators were permitted, even encouraged, to consult other popular English translations—Tyndale's Bible, the Great Bible, even the controversial Geneva Bible. But, King James insisted, this new Bible, being for all people, would contain no divisive commentary notes—only the biblical text.

Translators were instructed to work individually in rendering each section of Scripture. When they were done, they were to come together, compare notes, confer, and reach consensus on the final wording of the text. Once each book was translated in this manner, it was sent to the other committees for review and feedback.

The going was slow. The project took years because of its scope—and also because scholars are precise and picky. This meant the gatherings occasionally got tense. Personalities clashed.

One of the eight-man teams that convened in Cambridge, England, in 1604 was a collection of brilliant and quirky characters.

The appointed leader was Edward Lively, a humble, mild-mannered professor of Hebrew at Cambridge. In the years leading up to this royal project, Lively had lost his wife and two of his thirteen children. Because of such tragedies and chronic financial struggles, a friend likened Lively to the biblical character Job. Who better, then, to lead a team in translating the biblical book of Job? And not only Job but nine other Old Testament books—the final five historical books of the Old Testament (1 and 2 Chronicles, Ezra, Nehemiah, and Esther) and all five Jewish poetical books (the aforementioned Job, plus the Psalms, Proverbs, Ecclesiastes, and Song of Songs).

Andrew Bing was a bright, lanky, friendly scholar not yet thirty years old. Roger Andrewes was the argumentative younger brother of Lancelot Andrewes (the director of a translation team that was working in Westminster). He was off-the-charts intelligent and also, according to author Adam Nicholson, "widely loathed."[4]

Two of Lively's team members were devout Puritans—Thomas Harrison and the elderly Laurence Chaderton (a charming, beloved preacher from a staunch Catholic background). John Richardson was a corpulent, well-to-do Hebrew scholar who vehemently disagreed with the Puritans' Calvinistic beliefs. Also in the group was the youthful William Eyre, Chaderton's former student, who was becoming more enamored with the traditional views of the Church of England.

The group dynamics here (and in all the groups) must have been something to behold.

Because of the rich elegance of the language in the King James Bible, there have been whispers that perhaps the great William Shakespeare played a secret role in crafting this great work.

The "evidence" that some conspiracy theorists like to point to is this:

- Shakespeare was 46 in 1611 (at least for part of the year), the same year the King James Bible was published.
- If you look at the Psalms (regarded by many as the middle book of the Bible), and specifically at Psalm 46, and if you count 46 words from the beginning, you come to the word "shake."
- If you count backward from the end of that same psalm—omitting the Hebrew liturgical command "Selah"—you come to the word "spear."

For those so inclined, that's all the "proof" needed to believe that Shakespeare helped created the King James Bible, and even "autographed" his work.

What such people don't have an answer for is how Psalm 46 in the Geneva Bible has the words "shake" and "spear" in almost exactly the same places. (And it was published four years before the bard from Stratford-upon-Avon was born!)

In 1611, after seven years of rigorous labor, the collaborative effort of these six committees rolled off the presses of Robert Barker, the king's printer. The official title was: "The Holy Bible, Conteyning the Old Testament, AND THE NEW; Newly Translated out of the Originall tongues: & with the former Translations diligently compared and reuised by his Majesties Speciall Comandement."

As book launches go, the release of the King James Version (KJV) Bible was, at best, disappointing—at worst, a disaster.

Critics found fault. Hugh Broughton, a brilliant Hebrew scholar who had been left off the translation team because of his disagreeable temperament, lambasted the "ill-done" work, saying it bred in him "a sadness that will grieve me while I breathe."[5] Lest anyone miss his bitter disdain, he added that he would sooner be torn to pieces by wild horses than recommend such a Bible to England's churches.

Some angry readers charged that the KJV was nothing but a plagiarized version of Tyndale's Bible. Others claimed it was almost identical to the Geneva Bible. To be sure, it wasn't an altogether new translation. It was a revision and reworking of the English Bible by comparing existing translations with the best available Greek and Hebrew texts of the time.

Sales of the KJV weren't great. Serious Bible readers continued to prefer the familiar Bishops' Bible or the Geneva Bible (with its helpful explanatory notes). Shockingly, even some of the KJV translators continued to use the Geneva Bible in their own ministries!

Over time, however, as more churches began to read from the KJV, it became more familiar, then more accepted, and finally truly beloved. As ministers preached from it, its language became part of England's societal fabric. Spurring this popularity was the fact that King James soon forbade the printing of the Geneva Bible in England. There's nothing like a good monopoly to crush the competition.

Certain phrases, either lifted verbatim from the KJV or slightly adapted, became part of everyday discourse. As we mentioned earlier, many of these expressions—*a voice crying in the wilderness, at their wit's end, the apple of his eye, the powers that be, you reap what you sow, wolves in sheep's clothing, salt of the earth*—are still common in English-speaking cultures today.

But the impact of the KJV isn't just that it furnished English speakers with some nifty phrases. For four centuries, both the faithful and the faithless have been touched and haunted by its literary and spiritual power. Few other books have spoken to the human condition or told of eternal mysteries in such soul-stirring ways.

In his book *The Learned Men*, Gustavus Paine quotes the cynical H. L. Mencken as saying the KJV's English is "extraordinarily simple, pure, eloquent, lovely."[6] More recently, the late, great atheist Christopher Hitchens, spoke of the KJV's "crystalline prose."[7]

Majestic and rich, never clunky and trite, the KJV has a lyrical, almost sublime quality. Its words dance and delight. Its sentences both comfort and pierce the heart.

Charles Merrill Smith and James W. Bennett were right when they called the KJV "perhaps the only significant work of art ever produced by a committee."[8]

Many think of the King James Bible as a decidedly Christian work. Few are of aware of the huge impact it has had in Jewish circles.

In the early nineteenth century, most American Jews were either unable to read Hebrew, or suspicious of existing English translations (including the KJV), or both. This reality prompted Isaac Leeser to publish in 1854 a new English translation of the Tanakh, which he called *The Twenty-Four Books of the Holy Scriptures*. Though many found fault with Leeser's work, it clearly sparked a surge in Bible reading among Jews.

In 1892, The Jewish Publication Society decided to create a popular new English rendition of the Hebrew Bible. Wanting to utilize the best English possible, they modeled it after the Protestant Revised Version, which was based on the King James Version.

The result was the Holy Scriptures (now referred to as the OJPS, or "Old Jewish Publication Society"). *Time* magazine hailed the work for turning the Bible "into fresh, understandable, contemporary language." Quickly this version became the source quoted in Jewish textbooks and cited in Orthodox, Reform, and Conservative prayer books. An illustrated version was even was sold door-to-door in Jewish communities.

In 1985, this beloved translation was replaced with the *JPS Tanakh* (NJPS). However, many Jews still maintain that the original version, the version influenced by the King James translation, is more lyrical and majestic.

Given the public's tepid reception to their new Bible, the men who came together to create the King James Bible never could have dreamed how much their work would alter the world.

And the idea that their translated and published prose would eventually be printed more than a billion times . . . and one day even visit the moon?

Unimaginable.

CHAPTER TWELVE

ON AND ON IT GOES

Wondrous Discoveries, Wider Distribution

Curiosity is the very basis of education and if you tell me that curiosity killed the cat, I say only the cat died nobly.

—Arnold Edinborough

We can't end a book about the "world's greatest book" without mentioning two remarkable women: Agnes Smith Lewis and Margaret Smith Gibson.

Talk about a dynamic duo! These twin sisters were forces of nature. They were Scottish Presbyterians who enjoyed the company of skeptics. They were self-taught scholars who liked a good party.

Hopelessly curious, the women were continually studying and learning. Endlessly adventurous, they were always on the go. More suited to the 1990s than the Victorian 1890s, Agnes and Margaret were the kind of fun, free-spirited women everyone wishes they had for an aunt or a fifth-grade teacher.

Agnes and Margaret never knew their mother, who died just two weeks after their birth. Their father, a well-to-do attorney and amateur linguist, never remarried. When his girls were young, John Smith made them a promise: each time they learned a new language, he would take them to the country where that language was spoken.

This arrangement resulted in lavish trips to Italy, Germany, Spain, and France. And so it was that John Smith's legacy to his daughters was a passion for travel and languages—they eventually mastered at least nine languages between them. Upon their father's death in their midtwenties, they also inherited his considerable wealth.

The sisters were always close. In adulthood, they became inseparable. According to Adina Hoffman and Peter Cole, "Agnes was the more ambitious, colorful, and domineering of the two; Margaret had a quieter intelligence."[1]

With ample time and money, these strong, independent women set out to master the biblical languages of Hebrew, Aramaic, and Greek. They supplemented their studies with field trips, traveling around the Middle East and Europe. They cruised the Nile. They explored Palestine. In 1870, Agnes published a book about their travels. In 1883, the sisters took a lengthy trip to Greece.

In their forties, both women "settled down." They married clergymen. Within a few years, both were widowed.

By the early 1890s, these linguaphiles had begun learning Arabic and Syriac (Christian Aramaic). As they did, they concentrated on two things: reports out of Egypt about old biblical manuscript discoveries and their long-term desire—in Agnes's words—to visit "the scene of one of the most astonishing miracles recorded in Bible history . . . the passage of the Israelites through the desert of Arabia and . . . the secluded mountain-top where the Deity first revealed Himself to mankind as a whole."[2]

So, when Rendel Harris, a Quaker friend, mentioned having seen a rare fourth-century manuscript called the "Apology of Aristides" during a recent trip to Egypt, the sisters responded predictably. They began packing their suitcases.

In 1892, they departed for the place every scholar wished to search in those days for old biblical manuscripts: remote Saint Catherine's Monastery at the foot of what many consider to be Mount Sinai. (Saint Catherine's, you will recall, is where Constantin von Tischendorf located Codex Sinaiticus in 1844—see chapter 1).

For the record, these adventurous sisters didn't exactly "rough it" in their trek across the Sinai desert. They hired a team of bedouin porters to lug their equipment and food supplies. Also, a chef and a butler were part of their retinue.

We have photos of these two plump, middle-aged sisters riding camels across the deserts of North Africa. Even better than that, we have the stories of their amazing discoveries.

Because of the Tischendorf affair—and a subsequent stream of document-obsessed scholars—the monks at Saint Catherine's were skittish. And, really, who can blame them for being protective of their old manuscripts? Agnes, however, hadn't come all that way for nothing. Turning on her considerable charm and utilizing her language skills, she eventually got one of the monks to show her some of the monastery's treasures.

One of the codices was very old. What's more, it was written in Syriac, the language Agnes was in the process of learning. It had, in her words, "a forbidding look, for it was very dirty, and its leaves were nearly all stuck together through their having remained unturned probably since the last Syrian monk had died centuries ago."[3]

As she examined this ancient work, she noticed something significant: the manuscript seemed to contain an upper writing and an underwriting. She remembered her father telling her and Margaret about how, when vellum was scarce, monks had been known to scrape away the older writing on the surface of a leaf so that they could write something new on top of it. Agnes had never before seen such a manuscript (called a *palimpsest*), but she realized at that moment she was staring at a very old one. The upper writing consisted of biographies of martyrs and saints, perhaps written about 700 CE. The faint underwriting appeared to be a text of the Gospels, at least 200 years older.

The sisters were allowed to take about 400 photographs of the palimpsest. Back in Cambridge, they and other scholars pored over the pictures. Two subsequent trips to Saint Catherine's confirmed the women's wild hopes: they had uncovered (literally) one of the earliest manuscripts of the Gospels ever found in any language. (It was definitely the oldest copy of the Gospels in the Syriac language.) This 358-page codex is now known as the Syriac Sinaiticus, a late-fourth-century manuscript of the Gospels.

If you think the sisters were done with their manuscript-hunting adventures, think again. They were only getting started.

By 1895, Agnes and Margaret were back in Egypt. Rummaging through the markets of Cairo, they purchased several intriguing manuscripts. One of their finds proved to be a leaf from an ancient palimpsest containing two layers of writing on a variety of previously used manuscript material. Careful analysis found that the several underwritings included portions of the Gospels in Greek—and, more importantly, in Palestinian Aramaic (dating from the sixth century). This was a landmark discovery because Aramaic is the language Jesus spoke.

The sisters suddenly had a new mission: finding and gathering all the leaves of this particular codex (now known as

Codex Climaci Rescriptus), and hopefully of finding other ancient texts. It took a decade, but Agnes was undaunted. From a German scholar/collector, she recovered eighty-nine leaves. The following year, in a port city near the Suez Canal, she came across and purchased about fifty more. Another page was discovered unexpectedly during a tour of the Westminster College Library in England! In 1909, Agnes was able to publish a translation of glimpses of the palimpsest.

The bulk of this codex now resides at the Museum of the Bible in Washington, DC—though some leaves are at Saint Catherine's, and two are at the University of Birmingham, England.

Perhaps you're wondering: *How is that even possible? It's one thing, in renovating an old house, to peel back tacky wallpaper and discover another layer (or two!) of even more hideous wallpaper underneath, but this is different. We're talking about scholars discovering and restoring layers of writing that have been scraped off or erased! Wouldn't that require something like Superman's X-ray vision?*

Almost. Thankfully, science and technology keep giving us better and more ingenious ways of reading texts that were utterly unreadable not so long ago.

In the 1890s, scholars like Agnes Lewis used chemicals (others even used mild acid) to erase the newer text of a palimpsest to reveal the older writing underneath. Sadly, this meant that the upper level of writing could be preserved only in transcription or photographically. At the time, these destructive techniques were considered cutting-edge science. And to a degree, they worked. However, as you might imagine, such practices routinely damaged (and sometimes destroyed) rare and fragile manuscripts.

Fast-forward to the 1950s. Sadly, things weren't a whole lot better. Well-meaning scholars and antiquities dealers, untrained in the delicate art of handling ancient texts, often pieced together darkened, tattered Dead Sea Scroll fragments with clear adhesive tape! They also put them under glass—not realizing that the sticky residue from the tape and the heavy weight of the glass were harming these priceless documents.

Since that time, however, pioneers in the field of ancient document study and preservation have borrowed technologies and adapted techniques from a host of other disciplines: physics, chemistry, biology, and photography.

Now an old manuscript discovery quickly resembles an episode of the popular TV show *CSI*. Microscopic fibers are examined forensically. Scientists conduct DNA testing on vellum leaves to discover if they came from the same animal skin and were possibly part of the same codex. High-resolution cameras are brought in. And because of advancements in digital imaging, computer processors, and web technology, scientists are now able to share, store, and access these stunning, crystal-clear images instantly.

It gets even better. With multispectral imaging, researchers can utilize different portions of the light spectrum to distinguish hidden layers of text. Want to read an erased and overwritten layer of text on an ancient palimpsest? No problem. Wish you could somehow differentiate unreadable dark text from the blackened scroll fragment on which it is written? Now you can with infrared imaging. The Museum of the Bible scholars, mainly working in partnership with Tyndale House, Cambridge, have transcribed the original text of Codex Climaci Rescriptus, once totally unreadable.

Case in point: In 1970, scholars found some burned parchment during a dig at Ein Gedi. Ein Gedi was a flourishing Jewish village on the western shore of the Dead Sea in the fourth through seventh centuries CE. But when the settlement and its synagogue burned, the inhabitants left, never to return. Thus, the Ein Gedi excavation proved to be an archaeologist's dream. At the site of the ancient synagogue, researchers found a charity box with coins still in it! They also dug up assorted oil lamps, found a menorah, and uncovered some charred scroll fragments. The glass and metal artifacts weren't hard to identify. The scroll fragments were a different story.

It took forty-five years, but technology eventually saved the day. Using state-of-the-art, high-resolution 3D scanning technology, scientists and scholars were able to identify the fragment as being a piece of the book of Leviticus from a 1,500-year-old Torah scroll.[4] Only the Dead Sea Scrolls are older! This scroll could not be unrolled, so they developed a sophisticated technique of reading all the layers of the burnt scroll and then "unrolling" the scroll by computer algorithms. Imagine what this kind of space-age technology will reveal when other ancient biblical fragments are scanned and studied!

By the way, thanks in large part to—who else?—Agnes and Margaret, we now have hundreds of thousands of manuscript fragments to analyze. You won't believe what those adventurous ladies did next.

The twin sisters were friends of Solomon Schechter, a Jew from Moldavia (now Romania) who happened to be a twin himself. Schechter had arrived in England in 1882 and taught himself English by comparing the Hebrew and English Bibles. He was a brilliant man, the quintessential absent-minded professor, with rumpled clothes, unkempt hair, and a scraggly beard. (He was also one of Cambridge University's most popular instructors.)

In May 1896, Agnes bumped into Schechter and began telling him excitedly about the manuscripts and document fragments she and her sister had recently purchased in Cairo. Since no one in Cambridge knew Hebrew like Schechter—he had reportedly memorized the Torah by age five!—Agnes asked if he would be willing to come by and take a look at what they had found.

In a flash, Schechter was at the women's home admiring the old manuscripts displayed on their dining-room table. The longer he looked, the more excited he became. After careful examination, Schechter gave the sisters stunning news: they were in possession of a piece of the apocryphal book Ecclesiasticus in Hebrew. No such manuscripts had been seen in almost 1,000 years!

As soon as possible, Schechter was en route to Egypt (with the assistance of Charles Taylor, an accomplished Hebrew scholar and Schechter's teaching colleague). He headed straight for the shops of

Fostat (Old Cairo), where the women had discovered their "manuscript gold." He eventually made his way to the Ben Ezra synagogue—the site, according to local legend, where the baby Moses had been found among the reeds.

It was there that the curious Schechter hit the jackpot. He had very good reason to believe that a storeroom (genizah) in this synagogue held a treasure trove of manuscripts that would change the entire field of Judaic studies. After impressing the synagogue leadership of the seriousness of purpose, he was allowed to enter the storeroom containing a tremendous number of old Jewish manuscript fragments! This trove of old documents, regarded as too sacred to be destroyed, was known to assorted scholars who occasionally perused its contents and published some of its manuscripts. Schechter, however, saw at once the great significance of this collection of materials, now known as the Cairo Genizah (*Genizah* being a Hebrew word, based on a Persian root, that means "repository, storeroom").

Schechter convinced the chief rabbi to let him sort through the mountains of dusty, fragmentary manuscripts. He eventually returned to Cambridge with more than 190,000 of these fragments. They are a wide array of religious and secular documents, dating from the late ninth century to the late nineteenth century. Name almost any obscure topic—early Yiddish literature, works of Arabic literature, Hebrew grammar studies, rabbinical commentary, ancient employee payment records, rejected versions of the Masoretic Text—and you probably can find a document about it in the Cairo Genizah.

The Genizah collection provided biblical scholars with manuscripts of Greek and Aramaic biblical translations, early Hebrew Masoretic texts, dictionaries and grammars of biblical Hebrew, Arabic, and other Bible translations, and Jewish biblical commentaries. This material has enriched immeasurably our understanding of the history of the dissemination and study of the Bible from antiquity virtually up to the modern era.

Can you imagine where the world of biblical scholarship would be without the relentless curiosity of people like Solomon Schechter, Agnes Lewis, and Margaret Gibson?

Or where the world of Bible distribution would be without the determination of ordinary people like Mary Jones?

Mary Jones, if you didn't know, is the fifteen-year-old girl who, in 1800, walked twenty-six miles (the distance of a marathon) just to buy a Bible from a Welsh Scripture salesman. This teenager's spiritual curiosity and determination led to the formation of the British and Foreign Bible Society. Over the next century, that organization gave away 180 million Bibles worldwide. In 1816, the American Bible Society was born. It not only *distributed* Bibles, but it also began *translating* the Bible for those who did yet have the Scriptures in their language.

Other groups have since joined in this task of trying to make the Bible available and accessible to everyone on the planet. According to statistics furnished by one of those entities—Wycliffe

Bible Translators—as of 2015, out of the 7,000 distinct languages spoken on earth, only 550 have both the Old and New Testaments. Some 750 more have all or part of the New Testament. Meanwhile, active translation work is underway in 2,300 additional languages. If you do the math, that leaves a huge number of distinct people groups still waiting for a Bible translation project to begin in their native tongue.[5]

Every Tribe, Every Nation is an alliance of like-minded organizations—the American Bible Society, Wycliffe, Biblica, The Seed Company, and SIL International—who have united in the effort to give people worldwide access to the Bible in their own languages.

Another group, One Hope, actively works to make the Bible available and understandable to children. A Bible they gave to a young girl in China in 2014 was the one-billionth copy of the Bible they have distributed.

Meanwhile, people around the globe continue downloading the You Version Bible app to their tablets and smartphones. As of this writing, You Version has been downloaded more than 200 million times (in more than 900 languages)—and counting!

While the above efforts have strong support from evangelicals, numerous robust efforts from different faith traditions also occurred to further Bible understanding. For example, Jews and Catholics have also emphasized the creation of commentaries, research works, archaeological projects, and a wide array of academic studies. And scholars from all these groups have been deeply involved in the planning, programs, and publications of the Museum of the Bible in Washington, DC.

Clearly, there is enormous interest in the Bible, and there are devoted groups eager to put it in the languages and hands of curious readers. Yet, even though the Bible is easily the most widely translated book in the world (still another reason it merits the title "world's greatest book"), more than a billion people are still unable to read it in their native language.

If we think again of Indiana Jones and *Raiders of the Lost Ark* (1981), one of the most iconic scenes is the discovery of the ark of the covenant, a key item in the Hebrew Bible. While the film is fictitious and intended only for entertainment, it captures the widespread awareness of the biblical narrative and the fascination with related artifacts. It is one of the highest-grossing films in history (around $400 million at the box office) and launched other movies, video games, and various products. The US Library of Congress National Film Registry included it (1999) for being culturally, historically, or aesthetically significant.

The Bible, from Genesis through Revelation, meets this standard on many fronts. Many phrases, names, stories, and key lessons from the Bible have become engrained in modern culture—and some of its teachings have had tremendous influence in shaping world history. *The Global Impact Bible* (Museum of the Bible, 2017) captures various aspects of this major influence. Numerous educational, religious, and personally funded efforts have studied these dynamics of the Bible's cultural influence. Likewise, these groups are often interested in scientific evidence that helps us to understand better this greatest of books—and here's where the archaeologists come in.

Many sources, such as the *Archaeological Study Bible* (Zondervan, 2006), provide insights from centuries of archaeological discoveries related to our understanding of the biblical narrative. Dr. Robert Cooley, President Emeritus of Gordon-Conwell Theological Seminary and veteran archaeologist, often states about archaeology's importance, "A text [the Bible], without a context [provided in part by archaeology], is just a pretext."

As we read through the Bible, we often wonder about the context of a story and become curious about what archaeologists have found that can provide this background. For example, 1 Kings 12 describes the worship of a golden calf at the city of Dan. Though archaeologists excavating the site have not found this calf, they have found numerous examples of cultic statues throughout the region from other population groups in Canaan. And, in 1993, they discovered at Dan one of the most important artifacts related to the biblical narrative: an inscription containing what many consider the earliest mention of King David, or more historically correct, the "House of David." Known commonly as the Dan Inscription, it's one of the main artifacts displayed at the Israel Museum. Not lost in this story is the reference to "House of David" and the amazing fact that the city of Dan itself was discovered—as is the case with a long list of other cities mentioned in the Bible.

Discoveries of the remains of the City of David are ongoing in Jerusalem and are forming a picture in line with the Bible story. Among many other significant finds is a massive fortress from the Davidic period. Many people have toured the adjacent interactive educational site and are learning about the homes of the common people and the Large Stone Structure, which is still being researched. The higher elevation of what noted archaeologist Eilat Mazar labels David's Palace may shed perspective on how King David likely had a view of people below, including Bathsheba bathing at a home or pool at a lower level (2 Samuel 11).

These finds are complemented by other significant discoveries, such as the Mesha Stele or Moabite Stone (840 BCE), which is slightly older than the Dan Inscription. It mentions King Omri of Israel, and some believe that line 31 of its text can also be read "House of David." But this is not the earliest reference to Israel outside the Bible. That's the Merneptah Stele—dating to around 1230 BCE.

The popular story of Samson razing the Philistine temple includes his supernatural strength, which is a matter of faith for any reader (Judges 16). However, have you ever wondered whether there were really Philistines? Hebrew Judges? Did temples with two central pillars exist among the Philistines? Archaeologists have found many Philistine cities, and in 1972 they uncovered a Philistine temple at Tell Qasile. In the middle of the structure are the bases of two pillars, about seven feet apart, that supported the upper structure. Tell Qasile is on the north side of modern Tel Aviv, which accords with the general location of Philistines in the biblical narrative, and the remains date to the general time of the events described in the biblical narrative. The find doesn't prove the miraculous part of Samson's story, but it does show the author's familiarity with buildings and the story's general context. But wait, there's more. In 2010, archaeologists from Bar-Ilan University found a similar temple (tenth century BCE) in one of the five Philistine cities—biblical Gath (Tell el-Safi). While neither temple seems large enough to hold 3,000 people as noted in the Samson account, these two sites give evidence of the two-pillar structure.

Excavations of Hittite sites, such as Hattusa (in modern Turkey), have helped us to understand more fully the Hittite presence early in the biblical narrative (Genesis 10). Egyptian and Hittite ancient records of the Battle of Kadesh show their military power, and numerous excavations make believable people's fear of the Hittites' military threat (2 Kings 7). The silver amulets found in a tomb at Ketef Hinnom (1979) contain a portion of the priestly blessing found in Numbers 6 and, at the very least, shows its religious significance to a family living in the sixth or seventh century BCE.

The excavations at Caesarea Maritima have helped us to understand the magnitude of Herod the Great's genius, revealing his ability to turn a shallow port into a thriving and necessary hub of international trade. There archaeologists excavated Herod's impressive theater, a lasting tribute not only to his massive building campaign but also to his immense power and economic strength. This theater is also the place in which the apostle Paul stood, according to Acts 24, before being sent to Rome for trial. Caesarea Maritima is also where, in 1961, archaeologists found the Pilate Inscription, the first extrabiblical evidence of Pontius Pilate, who figures prominently in the crucifixion account of Jesus in the Gospels.

Huge warehouses store archaeological artifacts related to biblical texts, and numerous museums worldwide exhibit others. The museum housing the Burnt House in Jerusalem is among the most educational for understanding first-century life in Jerusalem. It exhibits the house of the Katros family, one of twenty-four priestly families of the Second Temple period, nearly intact as the Romans destroyed it along with much of the city a month after they destroyed the temple (70 CE). Items there complement thousands of oil lamps, jars, tableware, and common utensils found at numerous other excavation sites.

The Israel Antiquities Authority (established in 1948) is the main repository of artifacts found in Israel. Research on its items helps scholars understand the daily life of the biblical period, thus illuminating the context of much of the Hebrew Bible and the New Testament, as well as of other early Jewish and Christian writings. The importance of these artifacts is manifested in the National Campus for Archaeology in Israel, along with its location between two museums on the edge of Jerusalem—the private Bible Lands Museum and The Israel Museum, which has the world's largest collection of biblical artifacts at its disposal, including the largest of the Dead Sea Scrolls.

It's inspiring, if not at times downright dazzling, to see scholars from various religious traditions collaborate on research and books in their quest for a greater understanding of the ancient biblical texts. Centuries of research have unearthed millions of archaeological artifacts. Libraries, research centers, professional organizations, and mega conferences provide opportunities for immense language knowledge and study efforts. Modern technology enables biblical scholars to interact daily around the globe.

Whatever any one of us might think about the Bible, it's clear that its importance manifests itself in many ways to the masses, in many cultures. And beyond the millions who read it daily (over 300 million on You Version alone), interdisciplinary studies by scholars from various backgrounds has led to a rich community of biblical scholarship.

Perhaps you have had the experience of watching an epic movie and finding yourself, at the end, too stunned to get up and leave. As the credits began to roll, you found yourself awed by something else. A single individual may have written and directed the film. But look at all those other names, all the varied and gifted people who came together to help make the story a reality.

The story of the Bible is not unlike this experience. The "cast and crew" behind the creation of the Scriptures features a few household names in the Western world, including Moses and Paul, William Tyndale and King James. It includes printing pioneers such as Gutenberg, Bomberg, and Soncino. But its production also includes a host of unknown scribes and unsung heroes from many cultures and centuries. Nameless record keepers, forgotten translators, goatherds, priests, nuns, monks, rabbis, heretics, lay scholars, smugglers, publishers. And most recently, technology geeks.

Put them all together and the result is a production unlike any other.

From the beginning, our goal for this book was to give a clear explanation of how the Bible came to be through sharing some of the remarkable stories surrounding the Bible's formation, transmission, translation, and dissemination.

Hopefully, you've had most of your basic questions about the Bible answered . . . and your curiosity aroused. If so—if you are asking new and deeper questions about the Bible, and if you desire to learn more about the origin or content of this one-of-a-kind book, then consider us delighted.

May we encourage you to do two things? First, check out one or more of the recommended resources listed at the end of this book. Second, at your earliest opportunity, see some amazing biblical artifacts for yourself at the new Museum of the Bible in Washington, DC. Located just three blocks south of the US Capitol, this eight-story, Smithsonian-quality museum features 430,000 square feet of interactive exhibits that tell many, many more fascinating stories and hard-to-believe anecdotes about the "world's greatest book."

APPENDIX

Tanakh (Torah, Nevi'im, Ketuvim)			Old Testament		
Law	Prophets	Writings	Pentateuch	Narratives	Wisdom Literature
Genesis	*Former Prophets*	Psalms	Genesis	Joshua	Job
Exodus	Joshua	Proverbs	Exodus	Judges	Psalms
Leviticus	Judges	Job	Leviticus	Ruth	Proverbs
Numbers	1 Samuel	*Five Scrolls*	Numbers	1 Samuel	Ecclesiastes
Deuteronomy	2 Samuel	Song of Songs	Deuteronomy	2 Samuel	Song of Songs
	1 Kings	Ruth		1 Kings	
	2 Kings	Lamentations		2 Kings	
	Latter Prophets	Ecclesiastes		1 Chronicles	
	Isaiah	Esther		2 Chronicles	
	Jeremiah	Daniel		Ezra	
	Ezekiel	Ezra		Nehemiah	
	Twelve Prophets	Nehemiah		Esther	
	Hosea	1 Chronicles			
	Joel	2 Chronicles			
	Amos				
	Obadiah				
	Jonah				
	Micah				
	Nahum				
	Habakkuk				
	Zephaniah				
	Haggai				
	Zechariah				
	Malachi				

Major Prophets	Minor Prophets	
Isaiah	Hosea	Nahum
Jeremiah	Joel	Habakkuk
Lamentations	Amos	Zephaniah
Ezekiel	Obadiah	Haggai
Daniel	Jonah	Zechariah
	Micah	Malachi

New Testament				
The Gospels and Acts	Epistles Attributed to Paul		Other Epistles	John's Apocalypse
Matthew	Romans	1 Thessalonians	Hebrews	Revelation
Mark	1 Corinthians	2 Thessalonians	James	
Luke	2 Corinthians	1 Timothy	1 Peter	
John	Galatians	2 Timothy	2 Peter	
Acts	Ephesians	Titus	1 John	
	Philippians	Philemon	2 John	
	Colossians		3 John	
			Jude	

ADDITIONAL BOOKS

Though various Bibles list these differently, these traditions usually include them within the main order of their books. For this chart's purpose, they simply are listed to show additional books within their lists, not separate categories.

Roman Catholic	Eastern Orthodox
Old Testament	
Tobit	1 Ezra
Judith	Tobit
1 Maccabees	Judith
2 Maccabees	1 Maccabees
Wisdom of Solomon	2 Maccabees
Wisdom of Sirach	3 Maccabees
Baruch (includes Epistle of Jeremiah)	Wisdom of Solomon
	Wisdom of Sirach
	Baruch
	Epistle of Jeremiah
New Testament	
None (no additional books)	None (no additional books)

NOTES

What's So Great About the Bible?

1. Alon Confino, "Why Did the Nazis Burn the Hebrew Bible? Nazi Germany, Representations of the Past, and the Holocaust," *The Journal of Modern History* 84, no. 2 (June 2012): 369–400, http://www.jstor.org/stable/10.1086/664662.
2. Roy P. Basler, ed., *Collected Works of Abraham Lincoln*, (New Brunswick, NJ: Rutgers University Press, 1953), 7:542; http://www.abrahamlincolnsclassroom.org/abraham-lincoln-in-depth/abraham-lincoln-and-the-bible/.
3. Origen, *Contra Celsus*, 4:43.
4. Mark Twain, *Letters From the Earth*, letter 3 (Seaside, OR: Rough Draft Printing, 2015), 19.
5. Ian McKellen, *Today*, interview with Matt Lauer, May 17, 2006, YouTube: https://www.youtube.com/watch?v=-IfYvFZjouA&feature=youtu.be.

6. "Jerome Completes the Vulgate," *Christian History*, http://www.christianitytoday.com/history/issues/issue-28/405-jerome-completes-vulgate.html.
7. H. L. Mencken, *Treatise on the Gods* (Baltimore, MD: The Johns Hopkins University Press, 1946), 205.
8. Kenneth Briggs, quoted in Emily McFarlan Miller, "Where Did the Bible Go? Author Finds 'Alternative Version of Christianity' in Mega-Type Churches," *Charlotte Observer*, September 8, 2016, http://www.charlotteobserver.com/living/religion/article100587007.html.

Chapter 1. In the Beginning: *Encounter at Sinai*

1. Codex Sinaiticus, "History of Codex Sinaiticus," http://codexsinaiticus.org/en/codex/history.aspx.
2. Dr. Dirk Jongkind, e-mail to Jerry Pattengale, May 8, 2017; see also Dr. Dirk Jongkind and Dr. Peter Williams, eds., *The Greek New Testament, Produced at Tyndale House, Cambridge* (Wheaton, IL: Crossway, 2017).
3. We get our English word *ostracism* from this word. In ancient Greece, pottery shards were used as tokens in voting whether or not to expel unwanted people from the community.
4. Bruce M. Metzger, *The Text of the New Testament: Its Transmission, Corruption, and Restoration*, 2nd ed. (New York: Oxford University Press, 1968), 43–44.
5. Codex Sinaiticus, "History of Codex Sinaiticus," http://codexsinaiticus.org/en/codex/history.aspx.

6. Ellen White, "Tischendorf on Trial for Removing Codex Sinaiticus, the Oldest New Testament," *Biblical Archaeology*, September 23, 2015, http://www.biblicalarchaeology.org/daily/biblical-topics/bible-versions-and-translations/tischendorf-codex-sinaiticus-oldest-new-testament/.

Chapter 2. People of the Book: *The Prophets and the Writings*

1. Dan Brown, *The Da Vinci Code* (New York: Anchor, 2009).
2. Tony Long, "July 4, 1776: Preserving the Declaration," July 2, 2009, *Wired*, https://www.wired.com/2009/07/dayintech_0704/.

Chapter 3. The Times They Are a-Changin': *Between the Testaments*

1. The other disputed writings—ranging from a few verses tacked on to an existing document, to whole new books—are Tobit, Judith, the Wisdom of Solomon, Ecclesiasticus (also known as Sirach), Baruch, the Letter of Jeremiah, 1 and 2 Maccabees, additions to the Book of Esther, some additions to Daniel (The Prayer of Azariah and the Song of the Three Young Men, Bel and the Dragon), 1 and 2 Esdras, the Prayer of Manasseh, and Psalm 151.)

Chapter 4. What the Goatherds Found: *The Dead Sea Scrolls*

1. Frank M. Cross, quoted in Hershel Shanks, *Freeing the Dead Sea Scrolls: And Other Adventures of an Archaeology Outsider* (New York: Bloomsbury Publishing, 2010), 133.

Chapter 5. "Gospel Truth": *Jesus and the Evangelists*

1. Elaine Pagels, *The Gnostic Gospels* (New York: Vintage, 1989), xxxv.
2. Edward Gibbon, *The Decline and Fall of the Roman Empire*, ed. J. B. Bury, 7 vols. (1896-1902), vol. 4. See esp. chapters 15–16, summarized in https://gbwwblog.wordpress.com/2013/10/27/gibbon-the-decline-and-fall-of-the-roman-empire-ch-15/.
3. Justin Martyr, *First Apology*, chapter 67; emphasis added.
4. Jerry Pattengale, "How the 'Jesus' Wife' Hoax Fell Apart," *Wall Street Journal*, May 1, 2014, https://www.wsj.com/articles/SB10001424052702304178104579535540828090438.

Chapter 6. Hatred and Heretics: *Assembling the New Testament*

1. Miles J. Stanford, *Foxe's Book of Martyrs*, ed. William Byron Forbush: (Grand Rapids: Zondervan, 1978), 29. This history of martyrdoms was first published in 1563.
2. Ibid.

Chapter 7. The Masoretes and Jerome: *Standardizing Scripture*

1. Paul Sanders, "Missing Link in Hebrew Bible Formation," *Biblical Archaeology Review* 41, no. 6 (November/December 2015), http://members.bib-arch.org/publication.asp?PubID=BSBA&Volume=41&Issue=6&ArticleID=4.

2. “Spreading the Word: Part 1,” The Smithsonian Institution, https://www.asia.si.edu/exhibitions/online/ITB/html/spreadingtheWord.htm.
3. Jerome, Vulgate, *Preface to the Four Gospels*, addressed to Pope Damasus (383).

Chapter 8. Light in the Darkness: ***Jewish and Christian Bibles in the Middle Ages***

1. Ezra Kassin, quoted in Matti Friedman, “The Continuing Mysteries of the Aleppo Codex,” *Tablet*, June 30, 2014, http://www.tabletmag.com/jewish-arts-and-culture/books/176903/aleppo-codex.
2. Joel Lovell, “Matti Friedman on the Unsolved Mystery of the Aleppo Codex,” The 6th Floor (blog), *New York Times*, August 3, 2012, https://6thfloor.blogs.nytimes.com/2012/08/03/matti-friedman-on-the-unsolved-mystery-of-the-aleppo-codex/?_r=0.
3. David Lyle Jeffrey, “Medieval Hebrew Bibles: Art and Illumination” in *The Book of Books*, J. Pattengale, L. H. Schiffman, and F. Vukosavoivic, eds. (Jerusalem: Bible Lands Museum, 2013), 66.
4. Jerome, Letter 22, To Eustochium, s. 32, from Latin, W. H. Fremantle, trans. (1892).
5. John Wycliffe, *On the Pastoral Office*, ed. and trans. Ford Lewis Battles, cited in Matthew Spinka, *Advocates of Reform from Wyclif to Erasmus*, vol. 14 of the Library of Christian Classics, J. Baille, J. T. McNeill, and H. P. Van Dusen, eds. (Philadelphia: The Westminster

Press, 1953), 49–51; see also John Wyclif, *Select English Writings*, ed. Herbert E. Winn (London: Oxford University Press, 1929).

Chapter 9. Mr. Gooseflesh's Revolution: *The Printing Press and the Bible*

1. Diana Childress, *Johannes Gutenberg and the Printing Press* (Minneapolis: Twenty-First Century Books, 2008), 62.

Chapter 10. Plow Boys, Women, and Girls: *Making the Bible Accessible*

1. John C. Olin, trans., *Christian Humanism and the Reformation: Selected Writings of Erasmus*, 3rd ed. (New York: Fordham University Press, 1987), 97.
2. "Erasmus," Christian History, http://www.christianitytoday.com/history/people/scholarsandscientists/erasmus.html.
3. Quoted in "Martin Luther," *Christian History*, http://www.christianitytoday.com/history/people/theologians/martin-luther.html.
4. Quoted in Mary Ann Jeffreys, "Colorful Sayings of Colorful Luther," *Christian History*, http://www.christianitytoday.com/history/issues/issue-34/colorful-sayings-of-colorful-luther.html.
5. Martin Luther, *Luther's Works*, Luther's Works (Augsburg) series (Minneapolis, MN: Fortress Press, 1960), 35:189.
6. Ibid., 35:193.

7. *Foxe's Book of Martyrs*, chapter XII, "The Life and Story of the True Servant and Martyr of God: William Tyndale," https://www.ccel.org/f/foxe/martyrs/fox112.htm.
8. William Tyndale, "To the Reader" (preface to the New Testament), 1526, http://www.bible-researcher.com/tyndale2.html.
9. Quoted in Bryan Edwards, "Tyndale's Betrayal and Death," *Christian History*, http://www.christianitytoday.com/history/issues/issue-16/tyndales-betrayal-and-death.html.

Chapter 11. One Billion Copies and Counting: *The Story of the King James Bible*

1. Fontenay, letter to Nau, quoted in Sidney Lee, ed., "James I of England," *Dictionary of National Biography* (New York: Macmillan, 1892), 29:163.
2. Adam Clarke, *The Holy Bible Containing the Old and New Testaments* (New York: G. Lane and P. P. Sandford, 1843), 1:14.
3. Michael Hattaway, ed., *A Companion to English Renaissance Literature and Culture* (Hoboken, NJ: Blackwell Publishing, 2000), 167.
4. Adam Nicholson, *God's Secretaries* (New York: HarperCollins, 2003), 253.
5. David Norton, *The King James Bible: A Short History from Tyndale to Today* (New York: Cambridge University Press, 2011), 185.

6. H. L. Mencken, quoted in Gustavus Paine, *The Learned Men* (New York: Thomas Y. Crowell, 1834), viii.
7. Christopher Hitchens, "When the King Saved God," *Vanity Fair*, April 1, 2011, http://www.vanityfair.com/culture/2011/05/hitchens-201105.
8. Charles Merrill Smith and James W. Bennett, *How the Bible Was Built* (Grand Rapids, MI: Eerdmans, 2005), 80.

Chapter 12. On and On It Goes: *Wondrous Discoveries, Wider Distribution*

1. Adina Hoffman and Peter Cole, *Sacred Trash: The Lost and Found World of the Cairo Geniza* (New York: Schocken Books, 2011), 3.
2. Agnes Smith Lewis, *In the Shadow of Sinai* (New York: Macmillan and Bowes, 1898), vii.
3. Ibid.
4. Daniel K. Eisenbud, "Most Ancient Torah Scroll Since Dead Sea Scrolls Found and Restored," *Jerusalem Post*, July 20, 2015, http://www.jpost.com/Israel-News/Culture/Most-ancient-Torah-scroll-since-Dead-Sea-Scrolls-found-and-restored-409586.
5. "Why Bible Translation?" Wycliffe Bible Translators, https://www.wycliffe.org/about/why.

GLOSSARY

Apocrypha. Ancient religious writings not universally accepted as part of the sacred canon.

Canon. (from the Greek word that means "standard or measuring stick") A collection of sacred writings recognized as Scripture.

Canonization. The process of determining which writings are sacred and binding for people of faith.

Codex. (plural, codices) An early form of the modern book in which the leaves (whether papyrus or parchment) are written on both sides and stitched together.

Epistle. A New Testament letter (of instruction, correction, or encouragement) written by an apostle to a Christian congregation or church leader.

Gospel. (from the Greek word that means "good news") A narrative about the life, teaching, and ministry of Jesus. The New Testament includes Gospels attributed to Matthew, Mark, Luke, and John.

Inspiration. The act by which God communicated holy thoughts and words to and through human authors. Such original writings are regarded as inspired or sacred.

Leaf. (plural, leaves) A page from a codex that features writing on both sides.

Manuscript. A document written by hand.

Masorah. The Jewish tradition of handing down holy texts with accuracy and precision.

Masoretes. The scholarly scribes in the seventh through tenth centuries CE who devoted themselves to the task of standardizing the Hebrew Bible.

Masoretic Text. The authoritative, standardized text of the Hebrew Bible.

Midrash. An ancient rabbinical commentary on part of the Hebrew Scriptures.

Mishnah. The definitive, written explanation of the Jewish oral law. The Mishnah comprises the first part of the Talmud.

Ostraca. Pottery shards on which ancient people wrote.

Palimpsest. (from the Greek phrase meaning "rubbed smooth again") A manuscript with text written on top of older, erased text.

Papyrus. A kind of ancient paper made from the pulp of an aquatic reed.

Parchment. The skin of sheep or goats which has been stretched, dried, rubbed, and cut so that it may be written on.

Pentateuch. (See Torah)

Scroll. A rolled document.

Septuagint. (also referred to as the LXX, the Latin number for seventy) A translation of the Hebrew Bible (Old Testament) into Greek made between the third and first centuries BCE. The name derives from the tradition that seventy-two scholars translated the Torah.

Talmud. The massive written collection of Jewish ceremonial and civil laws and traditions.

Tanakh. Hebrew term for the Hebrew Bible, derived from an acronym formed from the first letters of the titles of its three sections—the Torah ("Law"), the Nevi'im ("Prophets"), and the Ketuvim ("Writings").

Targum. An Aramaic translation and paraphrase of the Hebrew Bible.

Testament. A word meaning "agreement" or "covenant" that is employed by Christians to refer to either the Hebrew Scriptures (the Old Testament) or the Christian writings about Jesus and the church (the New Testament).

Textus Receptus. The Greek New Testament of Erasmus that was eventually used by Tyndale in creating his English Bible, and also in the development of the King James and New King James Bibles.

Torah. The first five books of the Hebrew Bible or Old Testament; also called the Pentateuch, Books of Moses, or the Law.

Uncial. A style of writing Greek or Latin popular in the fourth through eighth century, which features all capital letters.

Vellum. Fine parchment, usually calf skin.

Vulgate. Jerome's fifth-century translation of the Bible into Latin, the common language of the people.

RECOMMENDED RESOURCES

Akroyd, P. R. et al., eds. *The Cambridge History of the Bible*, 3 vols. Cambridge: University Press, 1969–73.

Archer, Gleason L. *A Survey of Old Testament Introduction*, updated and revised edition. Chicago: Moody, 1994.

Brettler, Marc Zvi. *How to Read the Jewish Bible*. New York: Oxford, 2005.

Bruce, F. F. *The Canon of Scripture*. Downers Grove, IL: IVP Academic, 1988.

Campbell, Gordon. *Bible: The Story of the King James Version*. New York: Oxford University Press, 2010.

Collins, John J. *Introduction to the Hebrew Bible*, 2nd edition. Minneapolis: Fortress, 2014.

Fields, Weston. *The Dead Sea Scrolls: A Short History*. Leiden, The Netherlands: Brill, 2006.

Friedman, Matti. *The Aleppo Codex*. Chapel Hill, NC: Algonquin Books, 2013.

Geisler, Norman, and William Nix. *A General Introduction to the Bible*. Chicago: Moody, 1986.

Harrison, R. K. *Introduction to the Old Testament*. Peabody, MA: Hendrickson, 2016.

Hoffman, Adina and Peter Cole. *Sacred Trash: The Lost and Found World of the Cairo Geniza*. New York: Nextbook/Schocken, 2011.

Metzger, Bruce Manning. *The Text of the New Testament*. 2nd ed. New York: Oxford University Press, 1968.

Pattengale, J., L. H. Schiffman, and F. Vukosavoivic, eds. *The Book of Books*. Bible Lands Museum, Jerusalem, 2013.

Reif, Stefan C. *A Jewish Archive from Old Cairo, The History of Cambridge University's Genizah Collection*. Richmond, Surrey: Curzon, 2000.

Sailhamer, John H. *How We Got the Bible*. Grand Rapids, MI: Zondervan, 1998.

Schiffman, Lawrence H. *Reclaiming the Dead Sea Scrolls, The History of Judaism, the Background of Christianity, and the Lost Library of Qumran*. New York: Doubleday, 1995.

Schiffman, Lawrence H. *From Text to Tradition: A History of Second Temple & Rabbinic Judaism*. Hoboken, NJ: Ktav Publishing House, 1991.

Sheler, Jeffery L. *Is the Bible True?* San Francisco: HarperSanFrancisco, 1999.

Smith, Charles Merrill and James W. Bennett *How the Bible Was Built*. Grand Rapids, MI: Eerdmans, 2005.

Tov, Emanuel. *Textual Criticism of the Hebrew Bible*, 3rd edition. Minneapolis: Fortress, 2012.

VanderKam, James and Peter Flint. *The Meaning of the Dead Sea Scrolls: Their Significance for Understanding the Bible, Judaism, Jesus, and Christianity*. New York: HarperCollins, 2002.

Yamauchi, Edwin M. and Marvin R. Wilson *Dictionary of Daily Life in Biblical and Post-Biblical Antiquity*. Peabody, MA: Hendrickson, 2017.

Würthwein, Ernst and Fischer, Alexander Achilles Fischer, trans. Erroll F. Rhodes, 3rd edition. *The Text of the Old Testament: An Introduction to the Biblia Hebraica*. Grand Rapids, MI: Eerdmans, 2014.